OLD-TIME STORIES

with illustrations
by
W· HEATH
ROBINSON

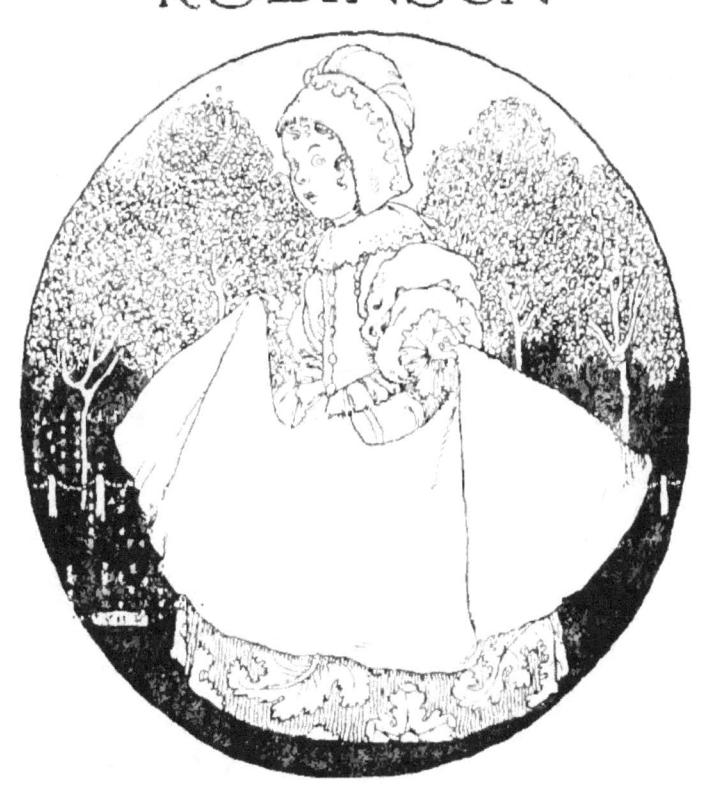

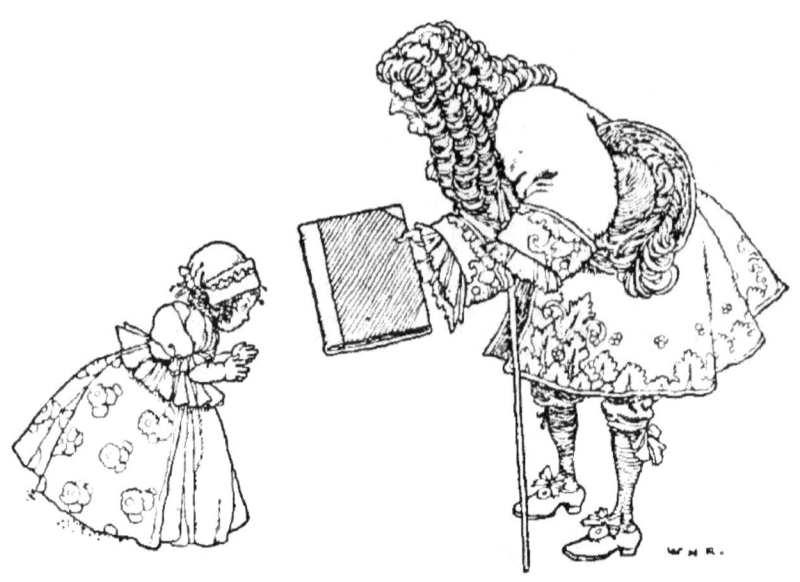

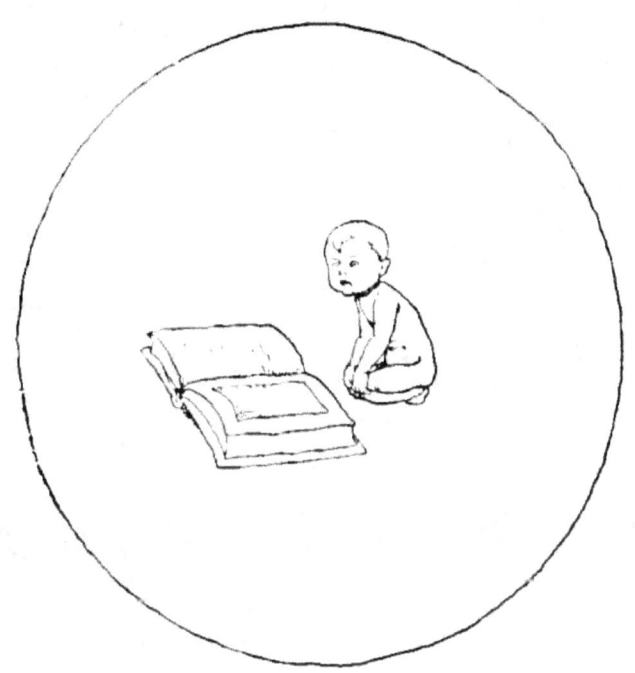

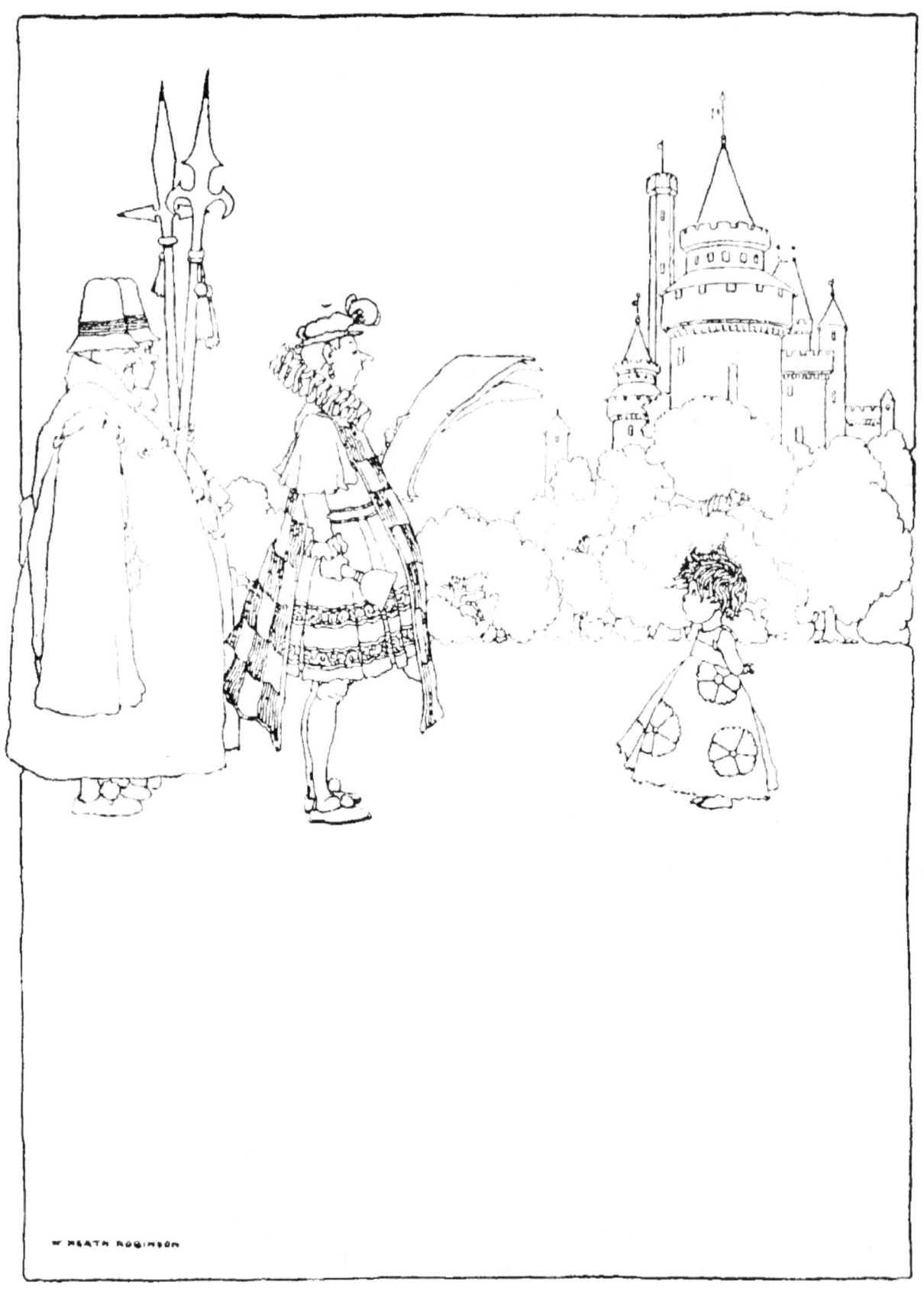

'The king . . . at once published an edict'

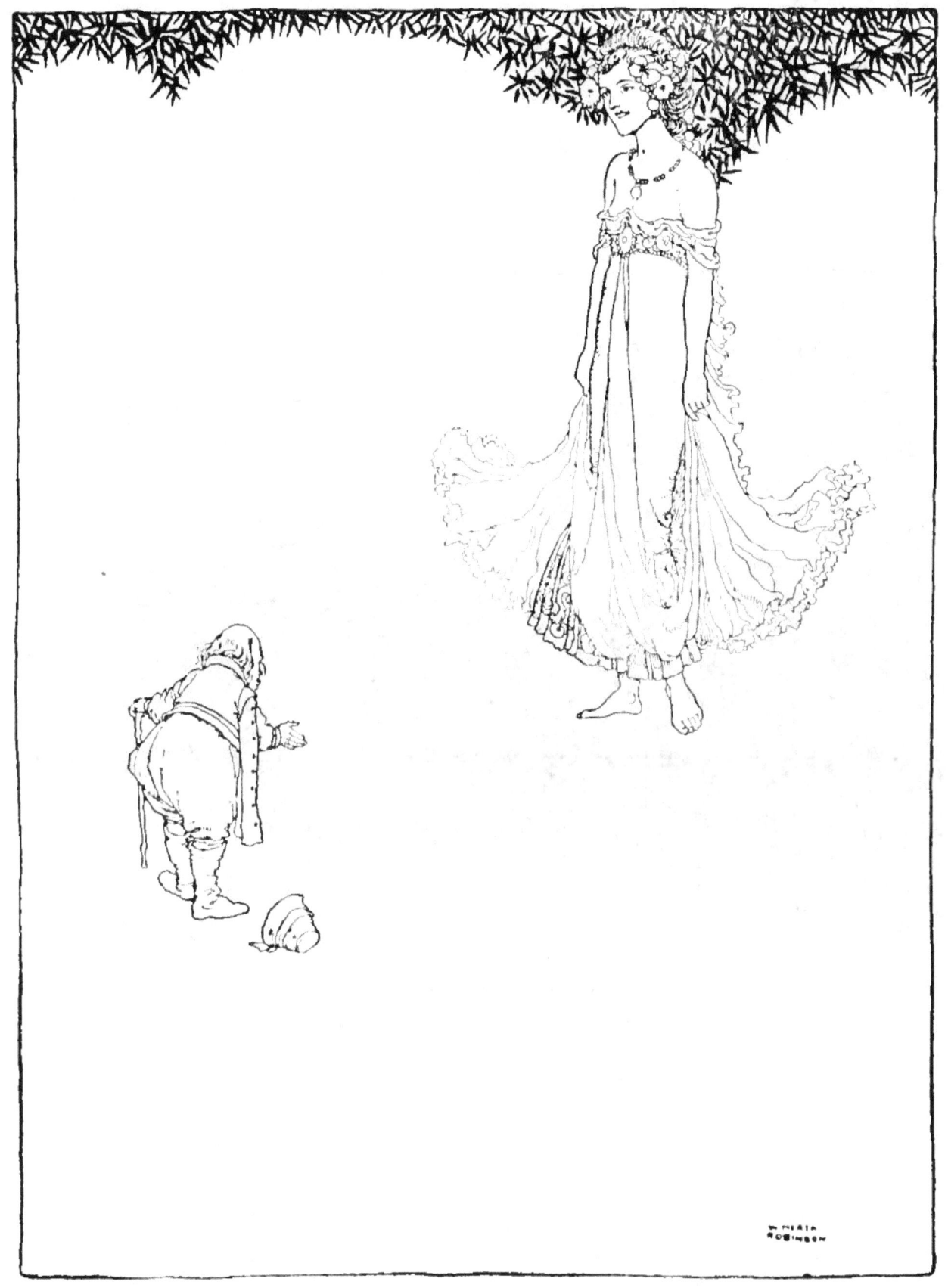

'*A little dwarf who had a pair of seven-league boots*'

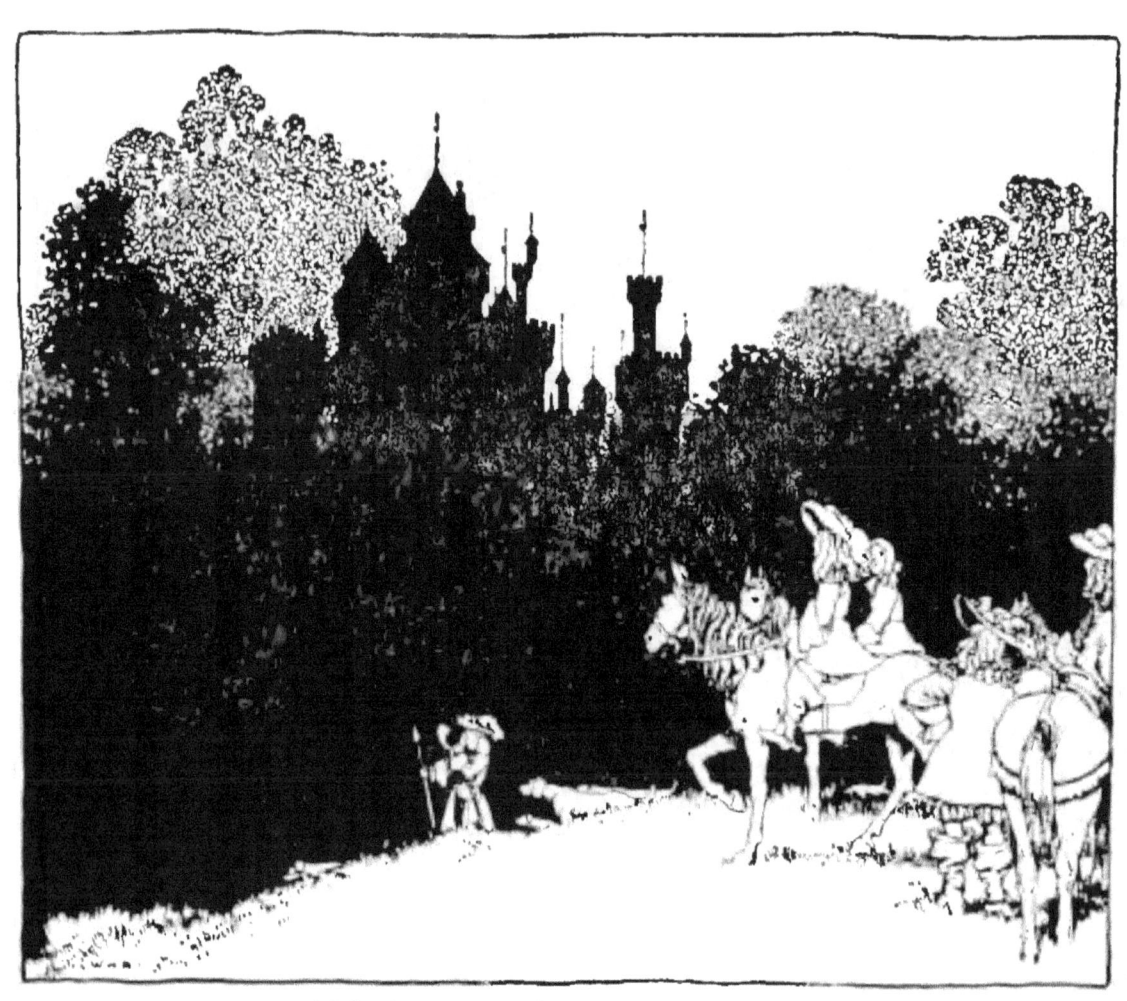
'The king's son chanced to go a-hunting'

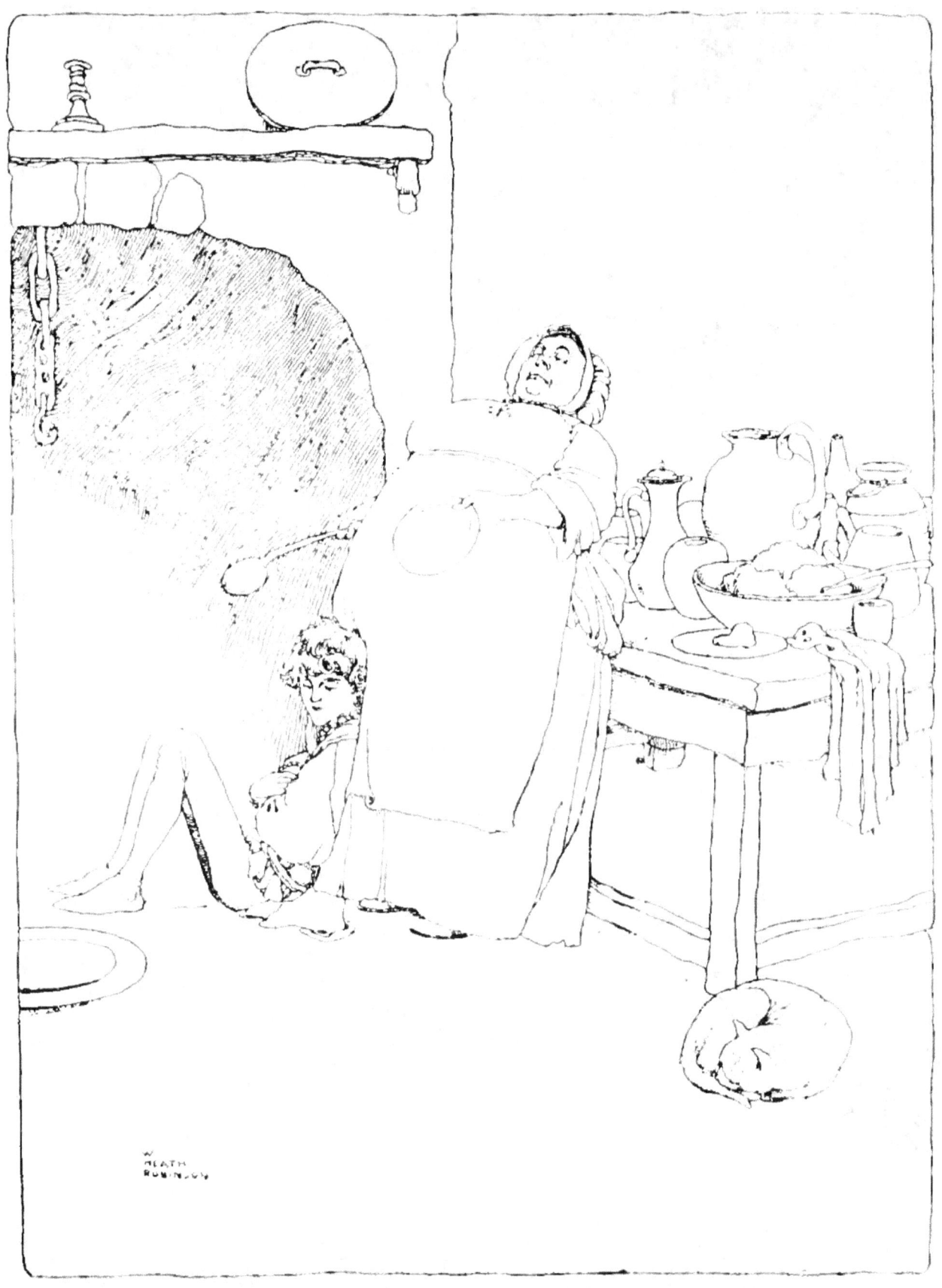

'They all fell asleep'

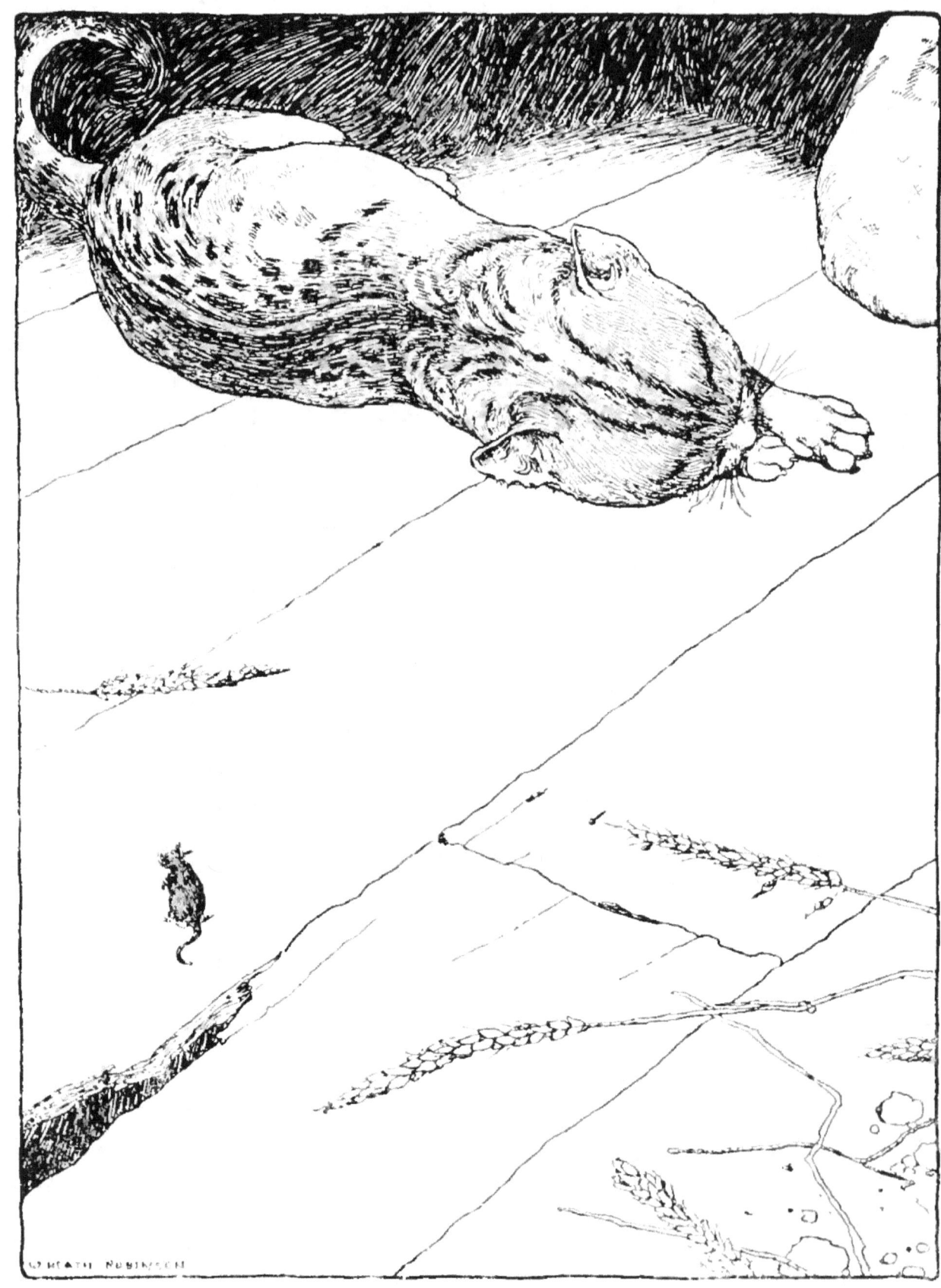

'As though he were dead'

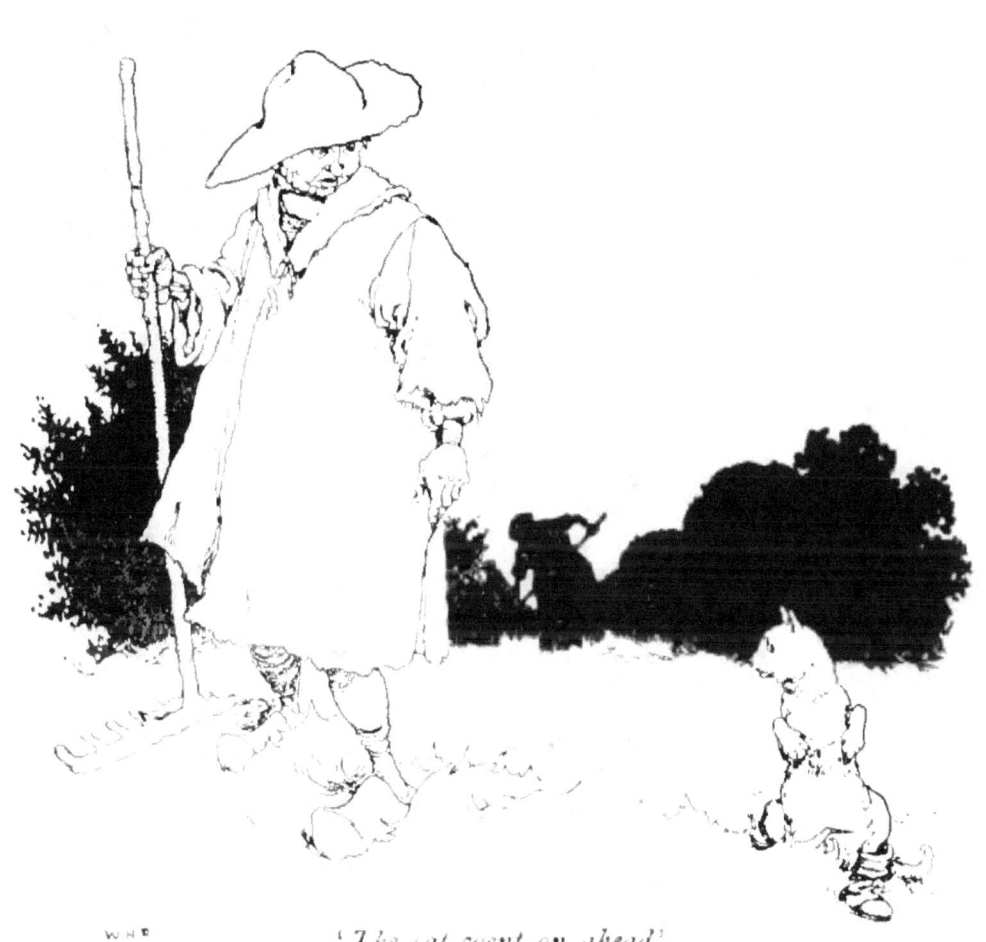
'The cat went on ahead'

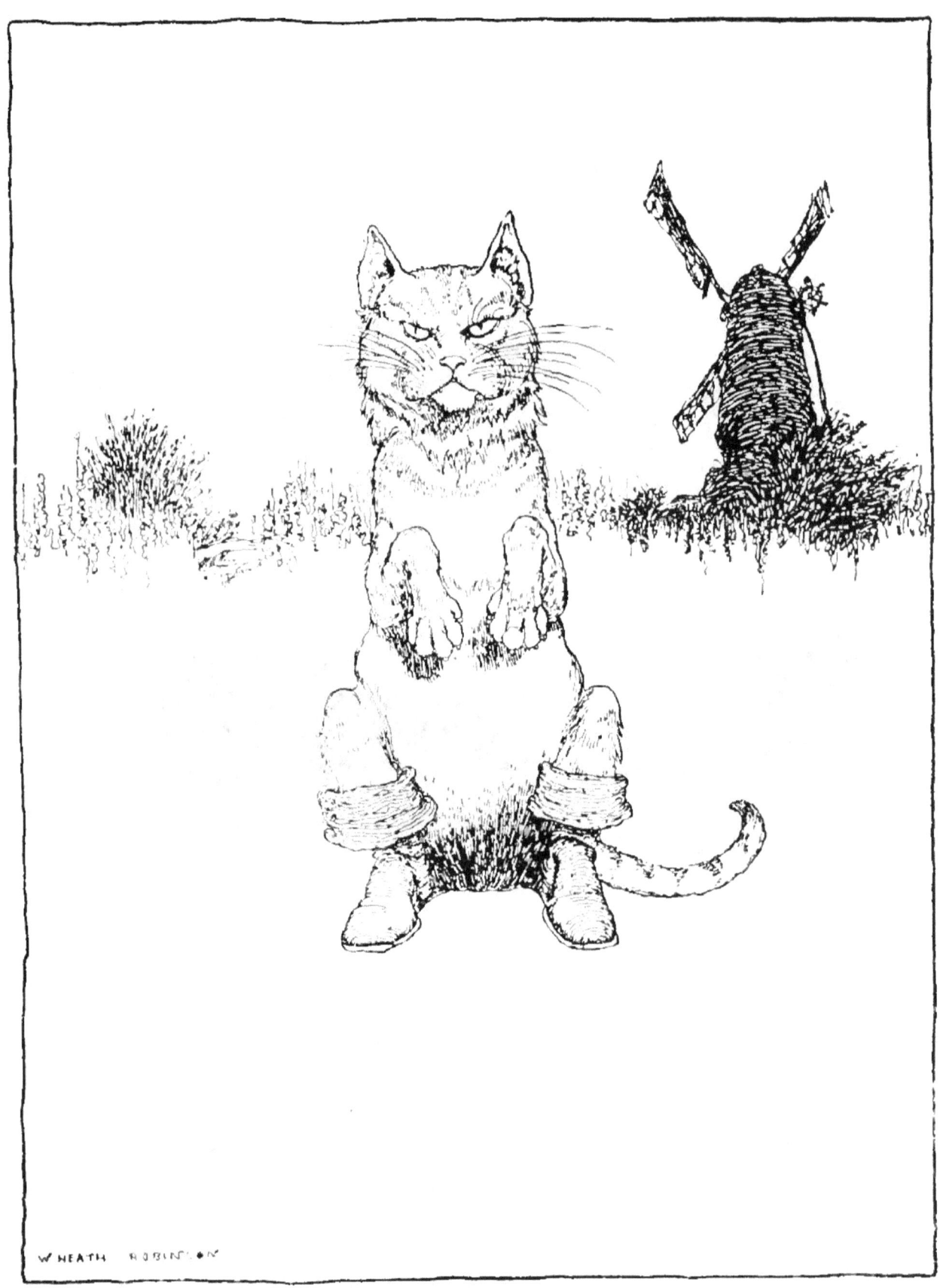

Puss in Boots

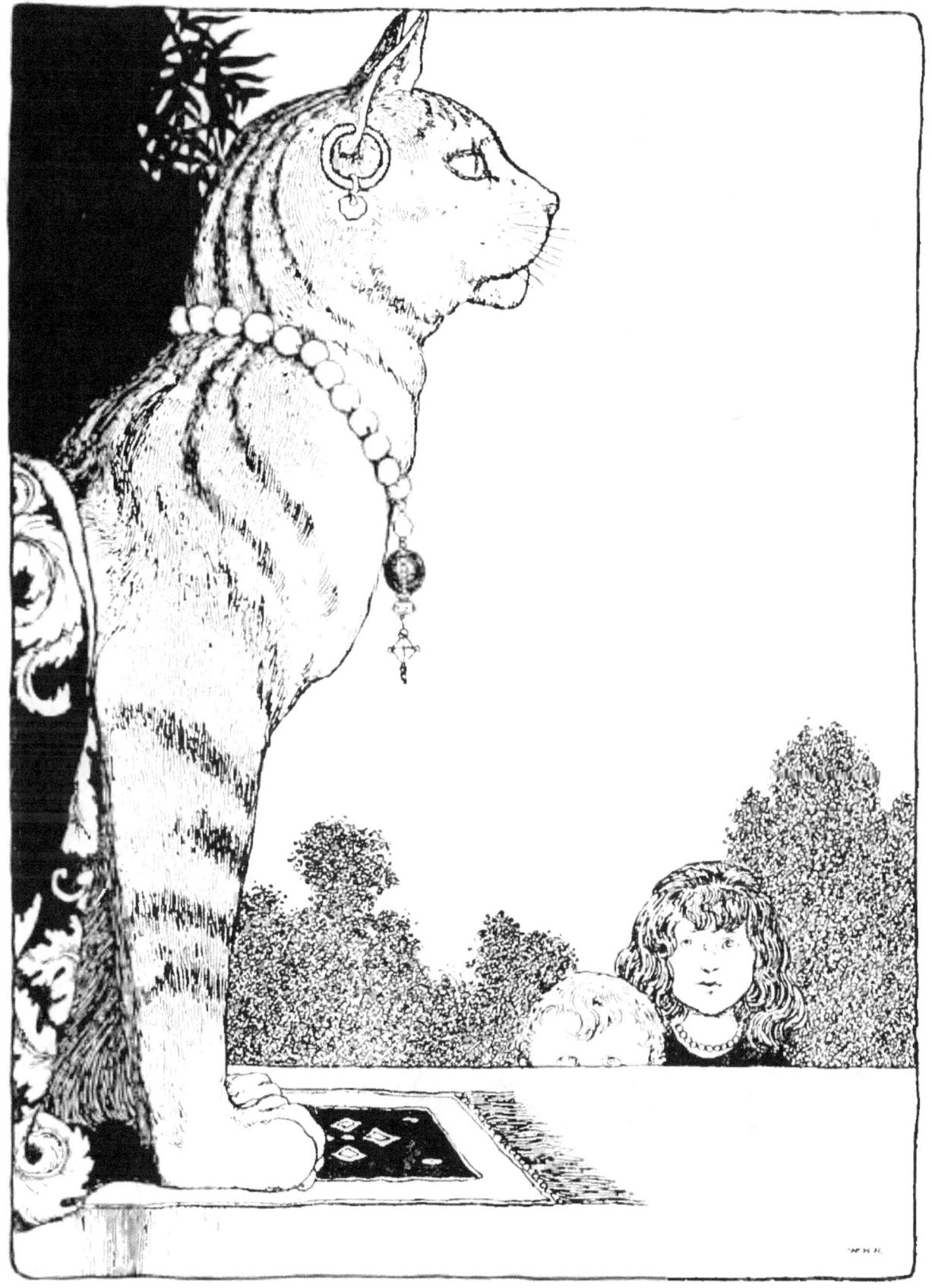

'Puss became a personage of great importance'

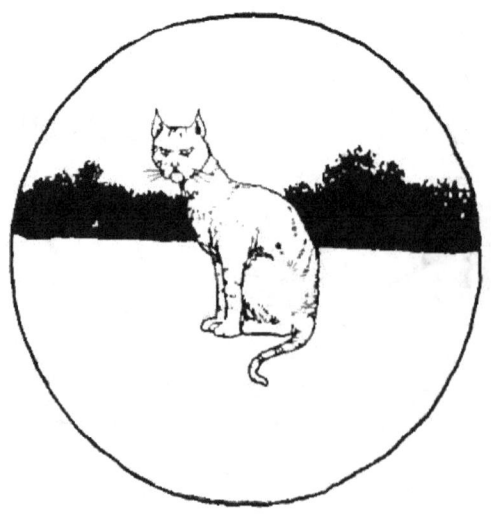

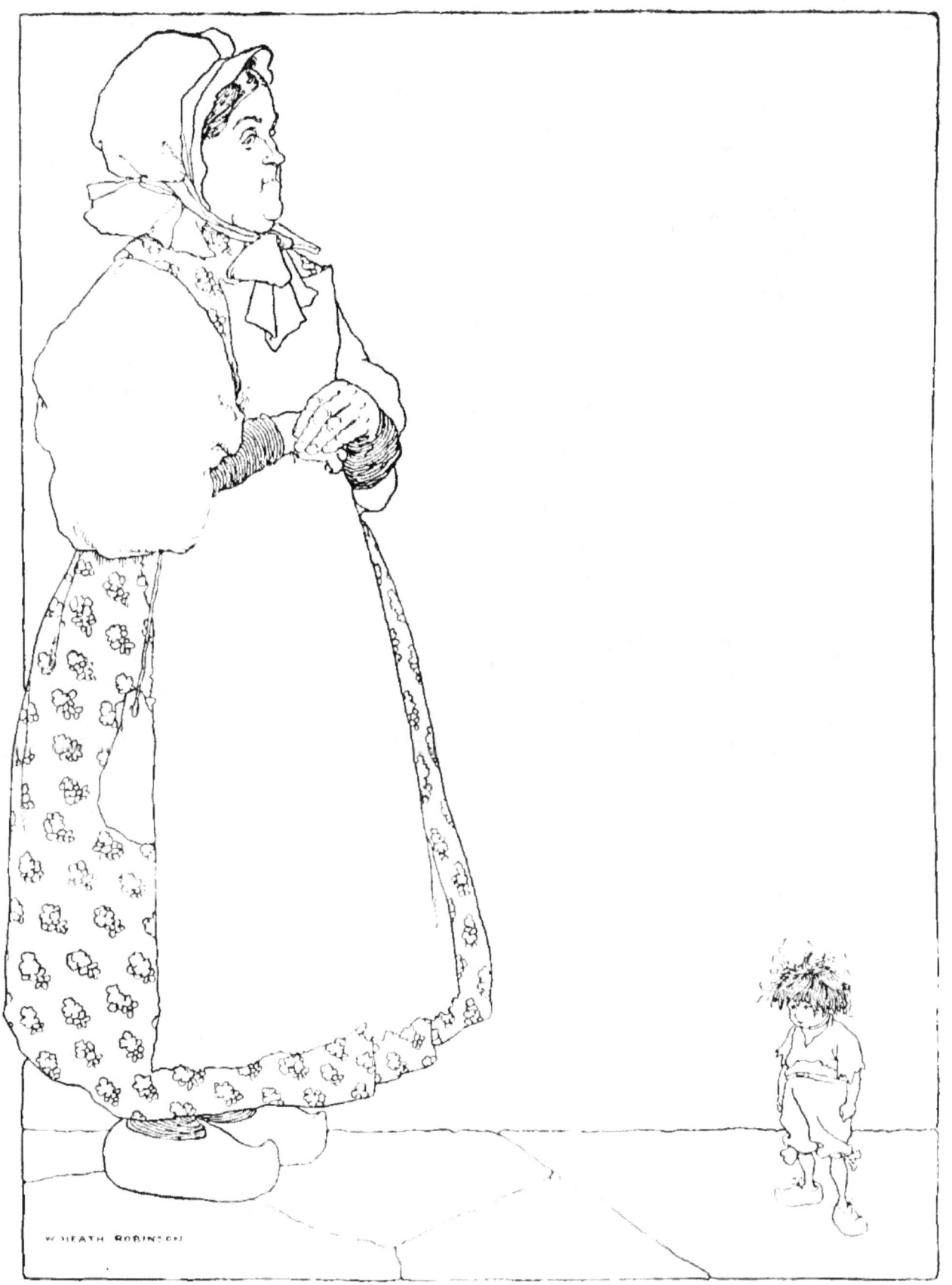

'*A good dame opened the door*'

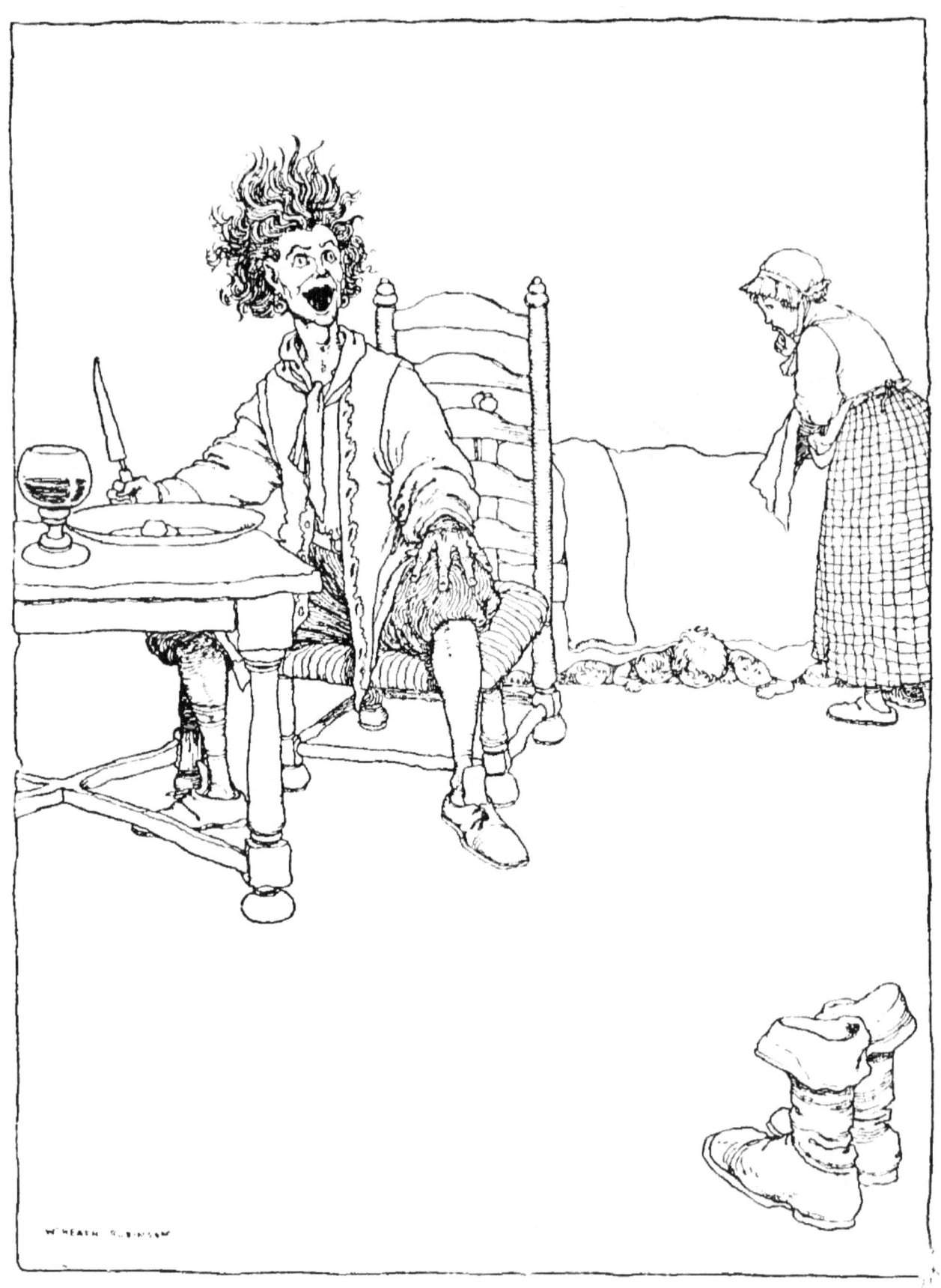

'He could smell fresh flesh'

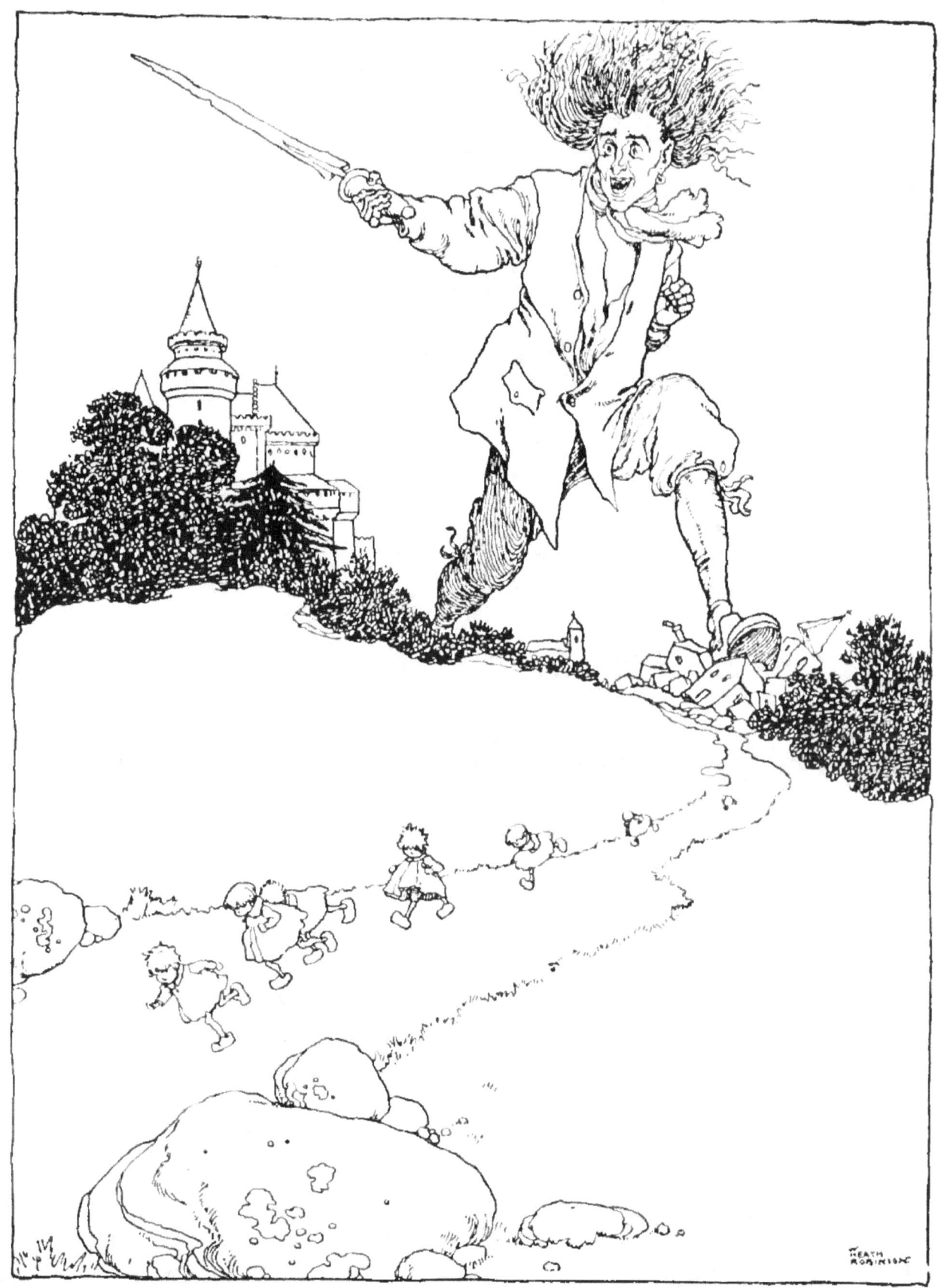

'*He set off over the countryside*'

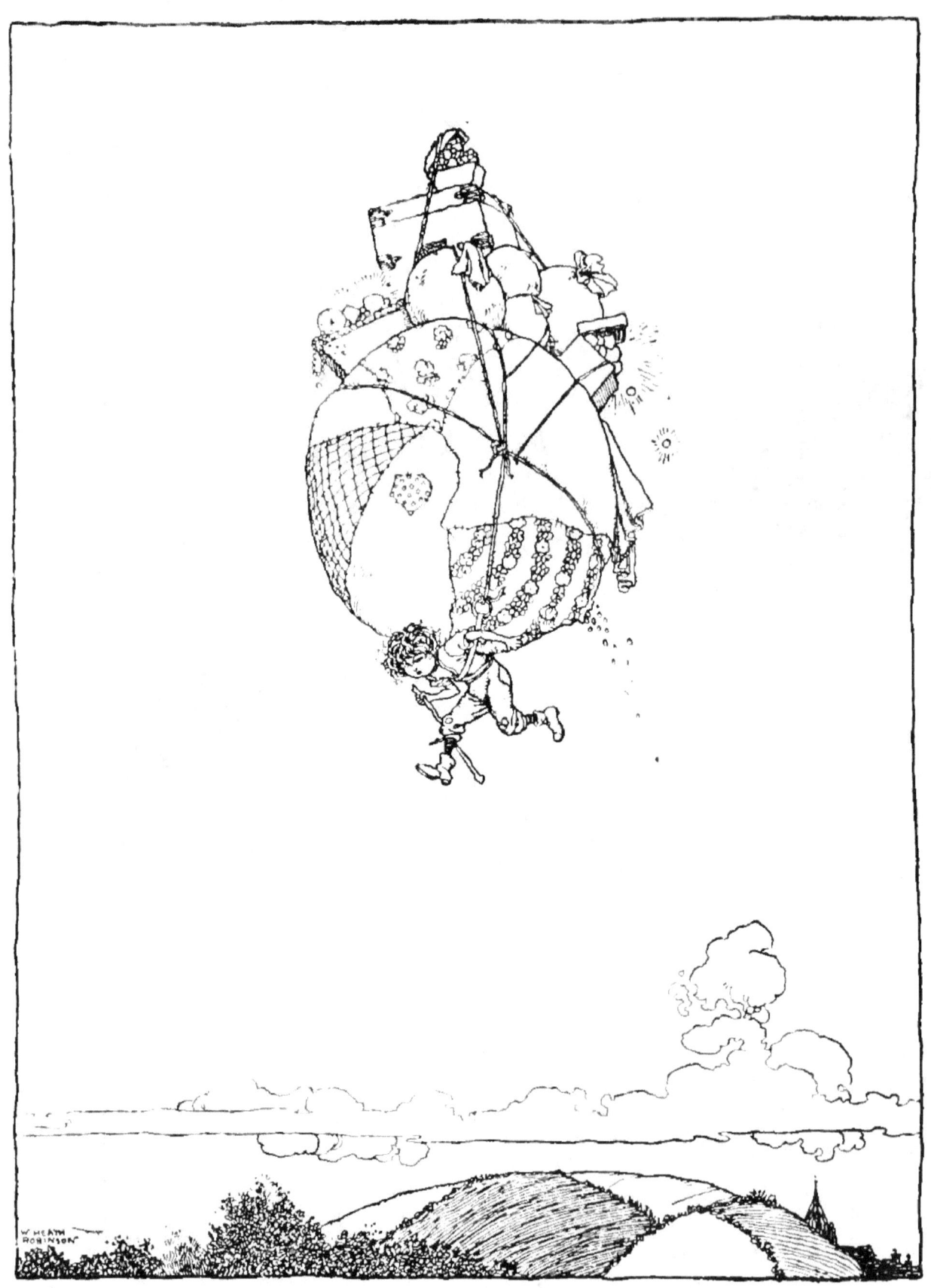

'Laden with all the ogre's wealth'

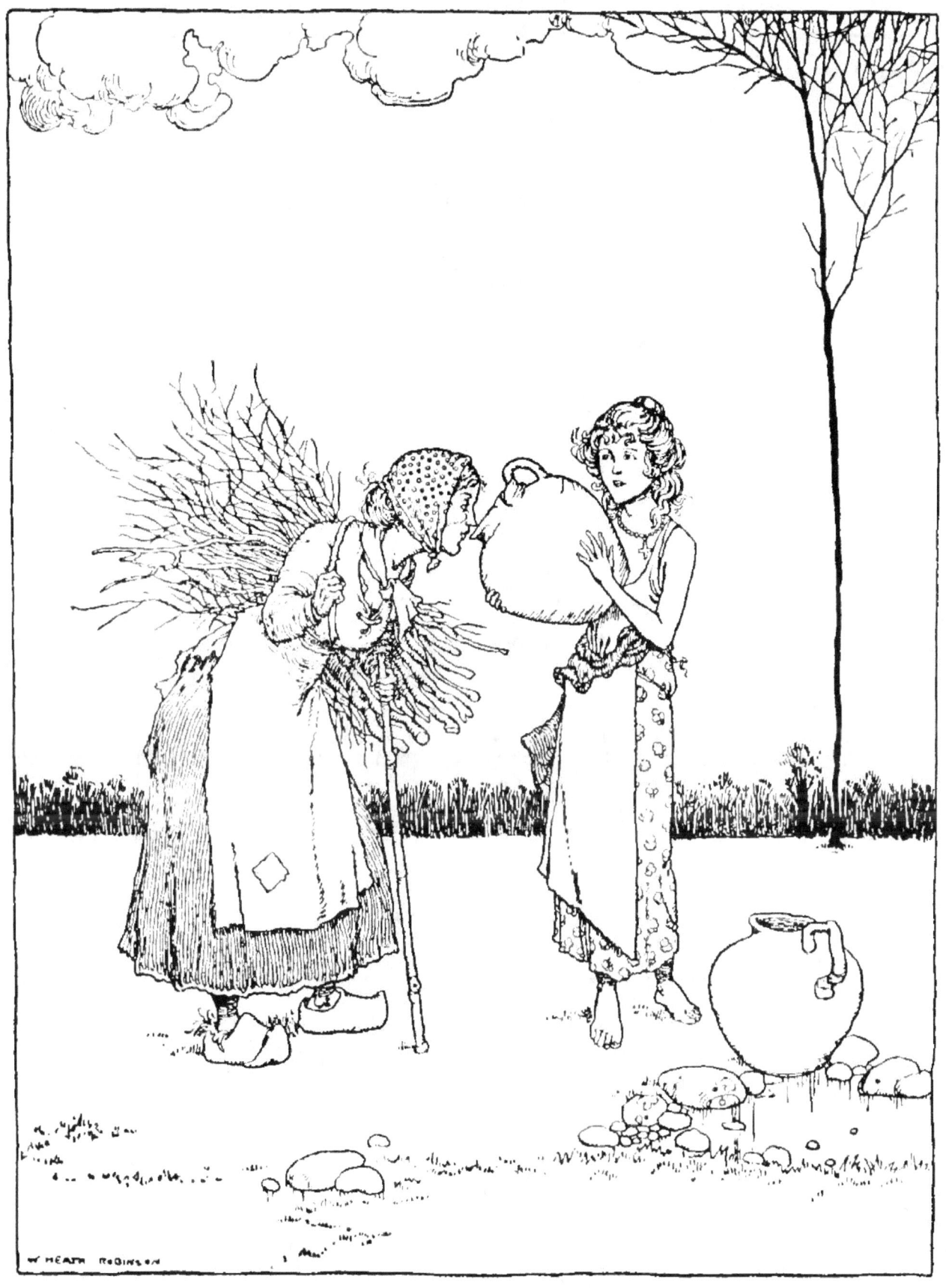

'Lifting up the jug so that she might drink the more easily'

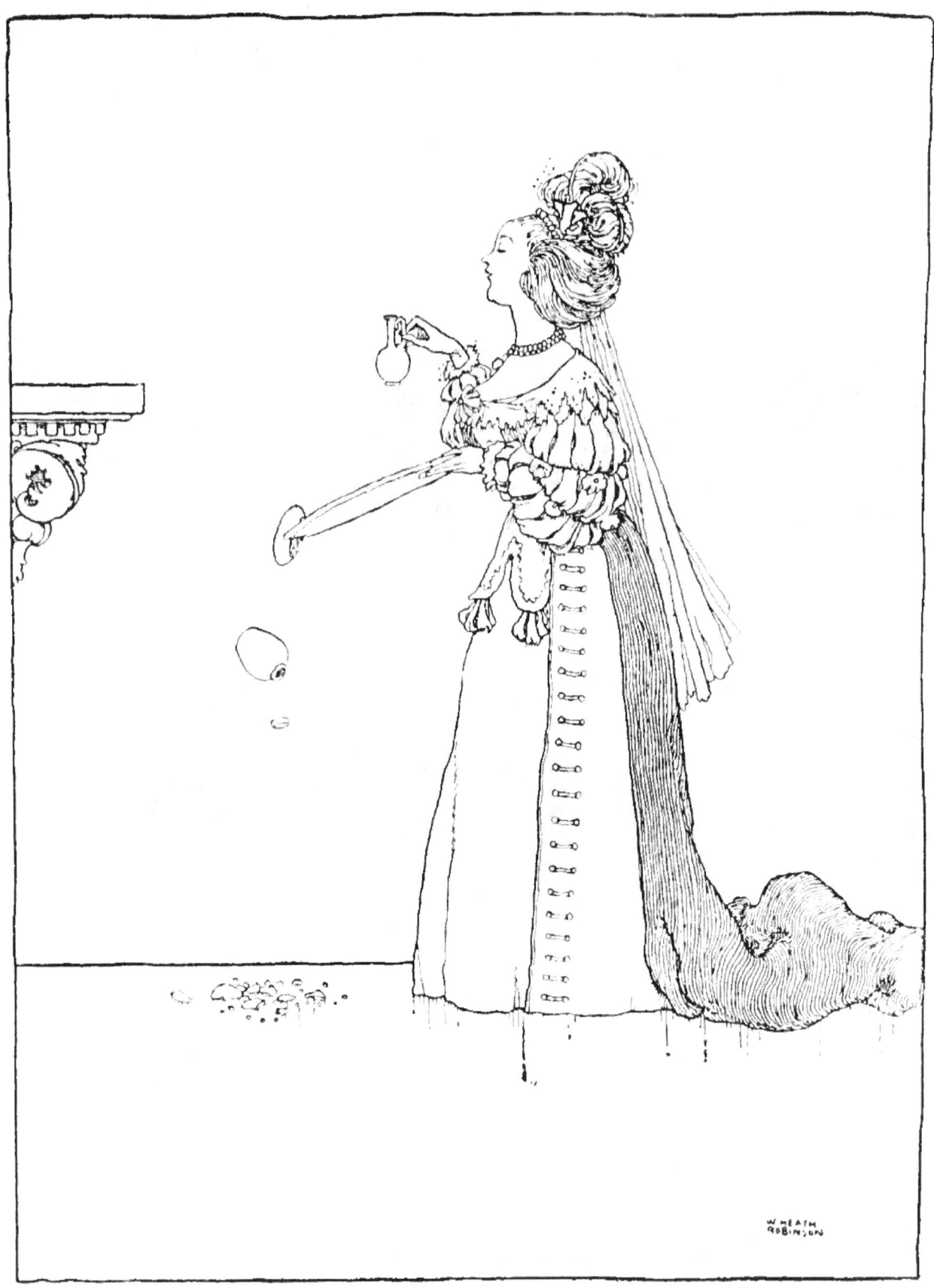

'*She could not set four china vases on the mantelpiece without breaking one of them*'

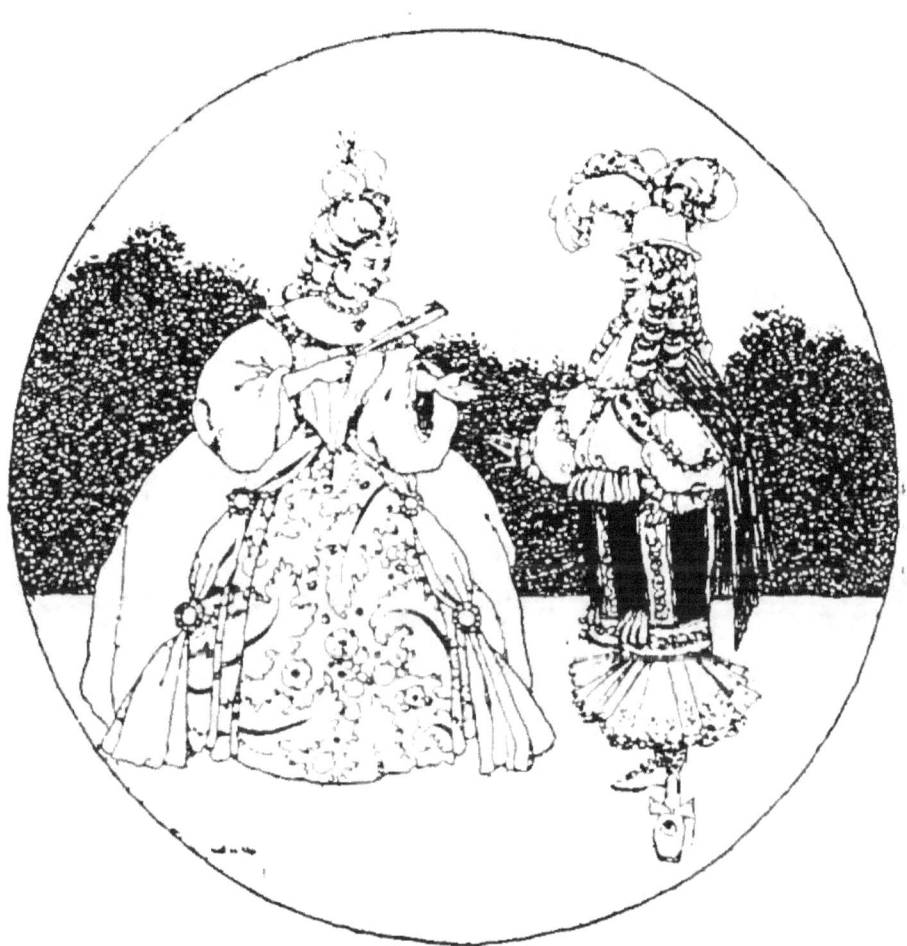

'Graceful and easy conversation'

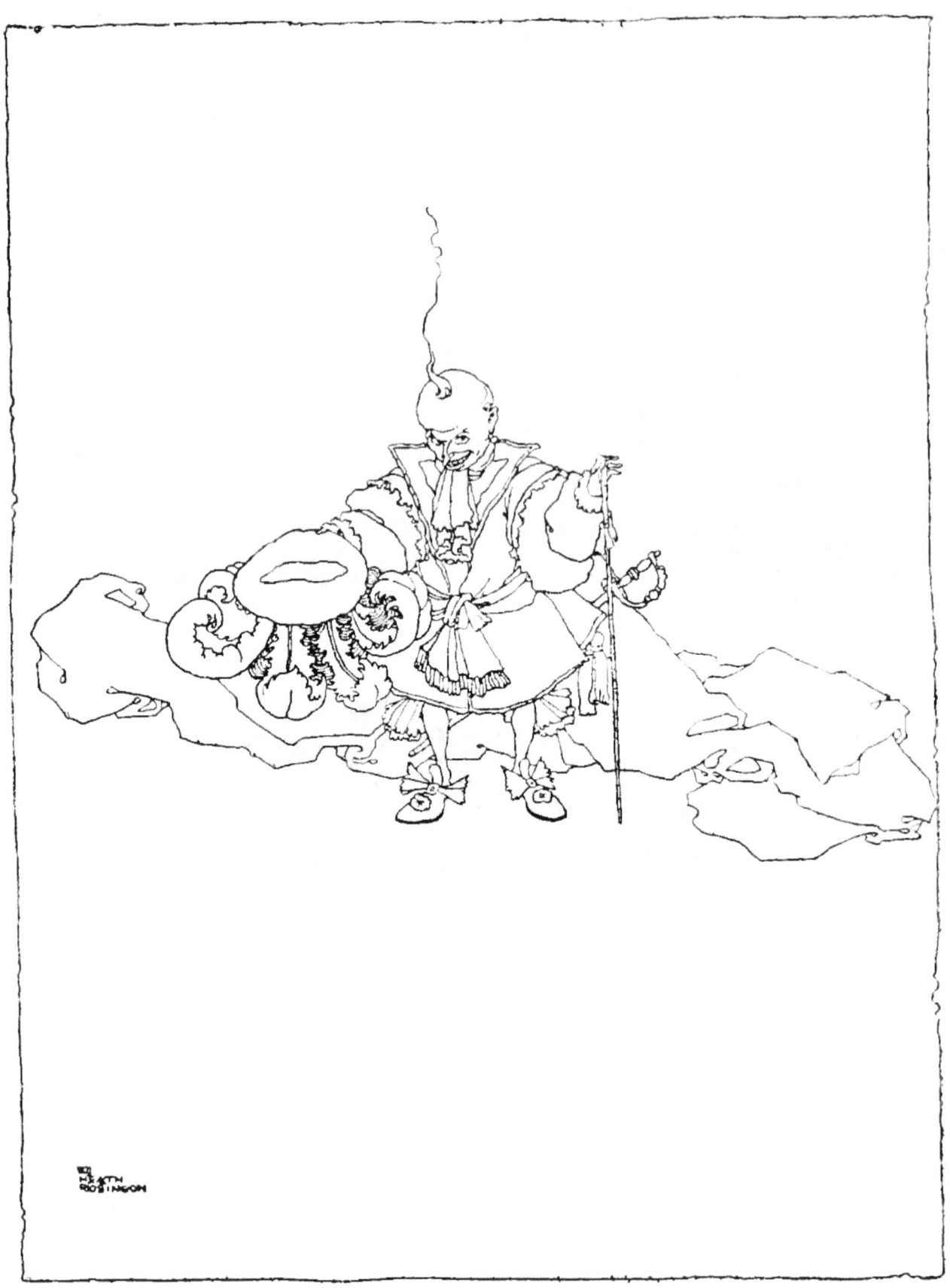

Ricky of the Tuft

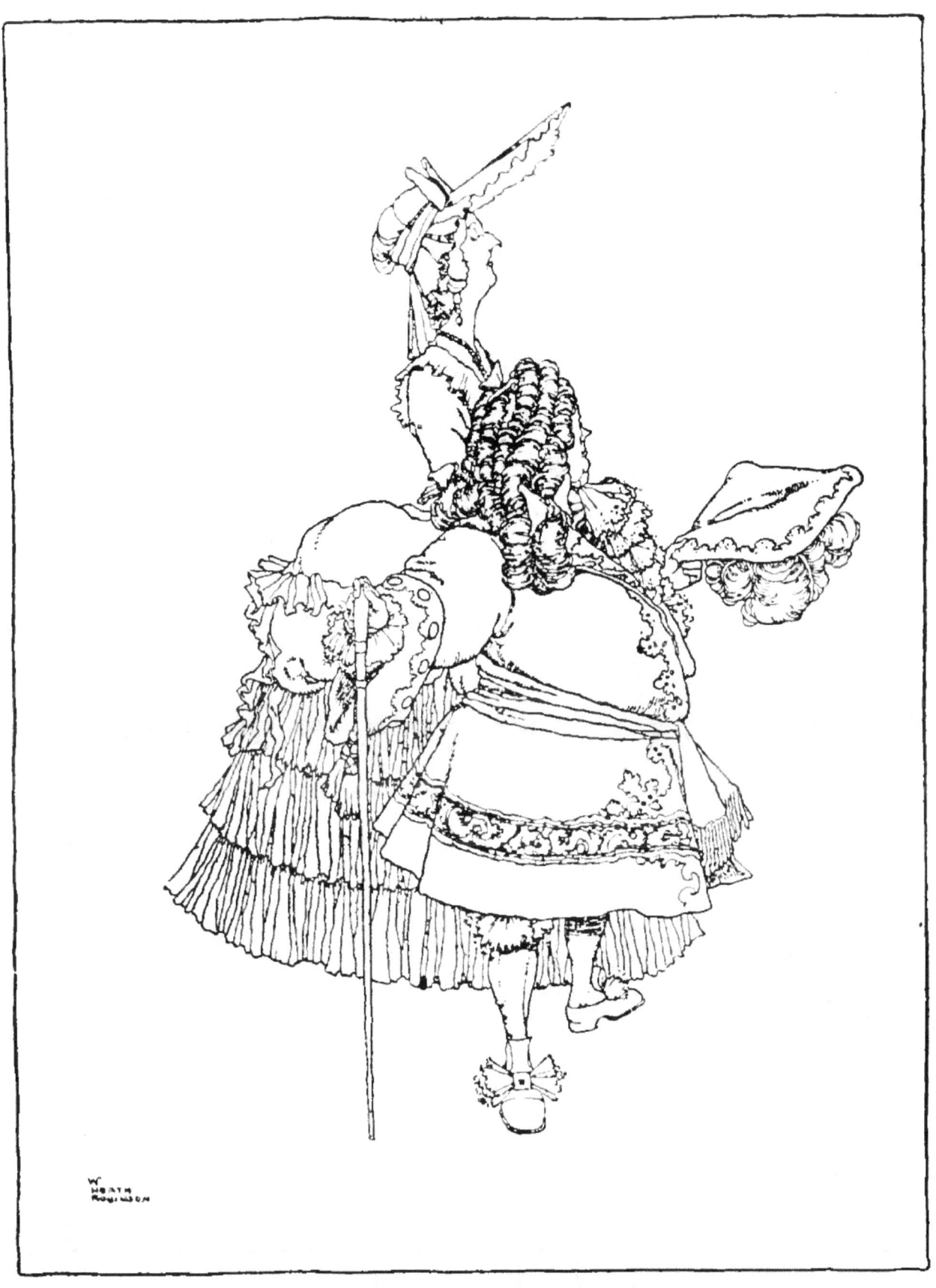

'*The haughtiest, proudest woman that had ever been seen*'

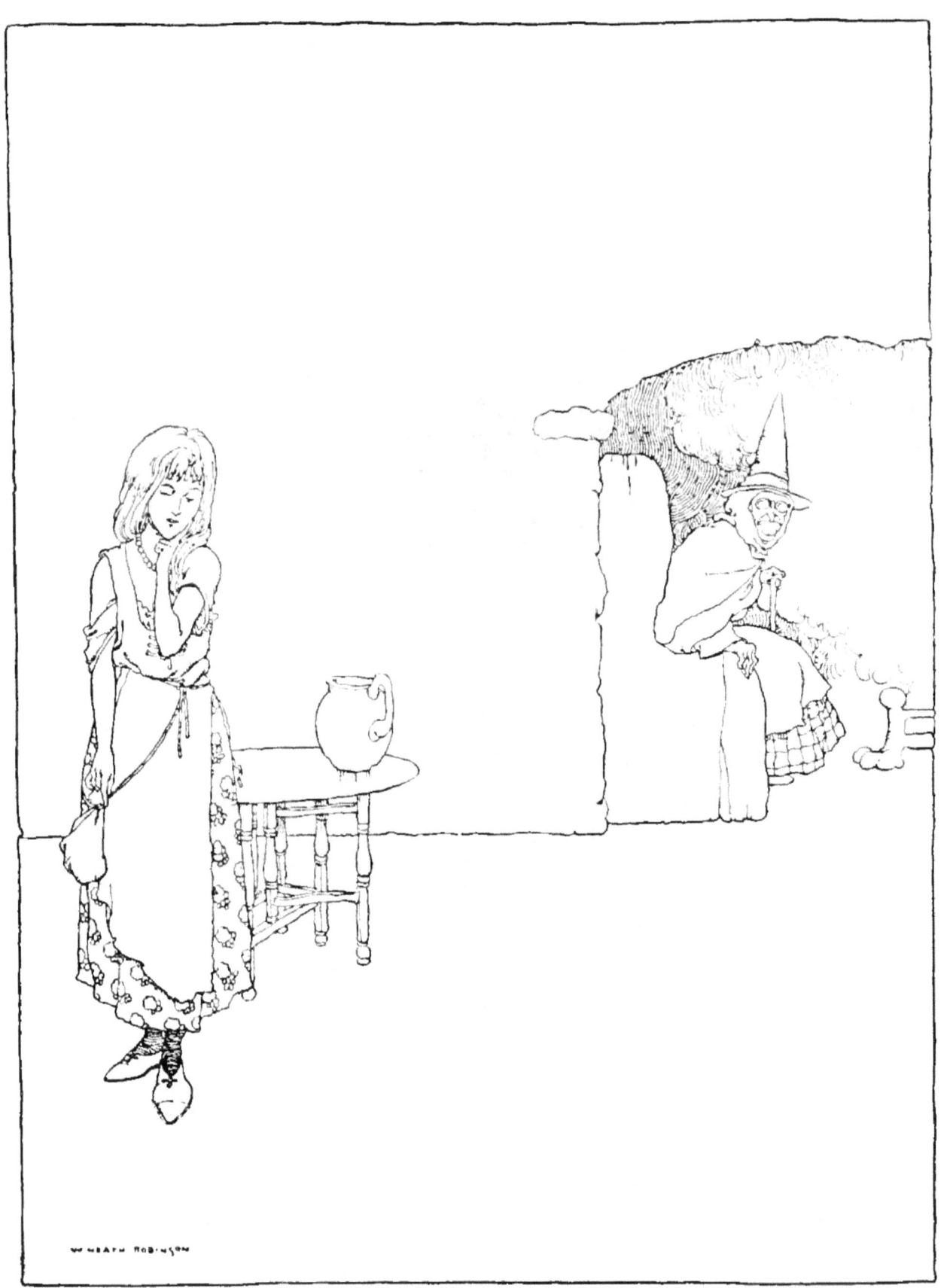

'Her godmother found her in tears'

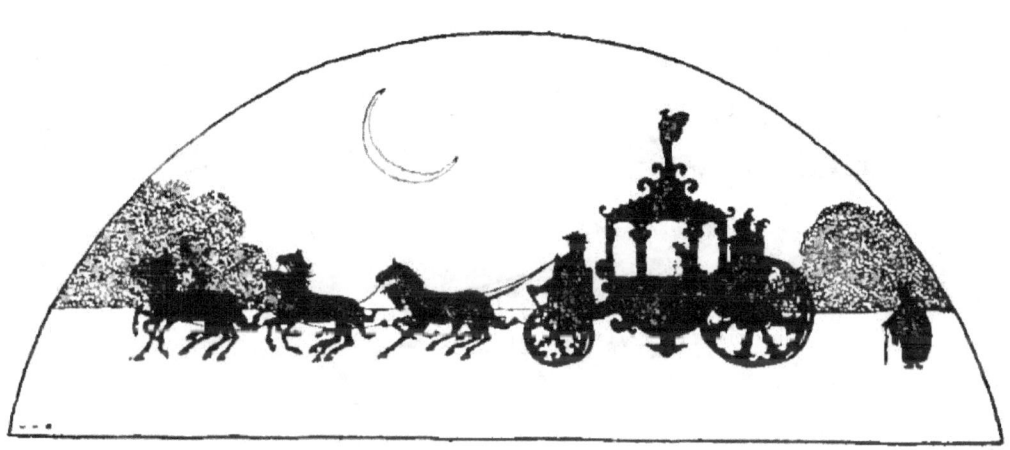

'*Away she went*'

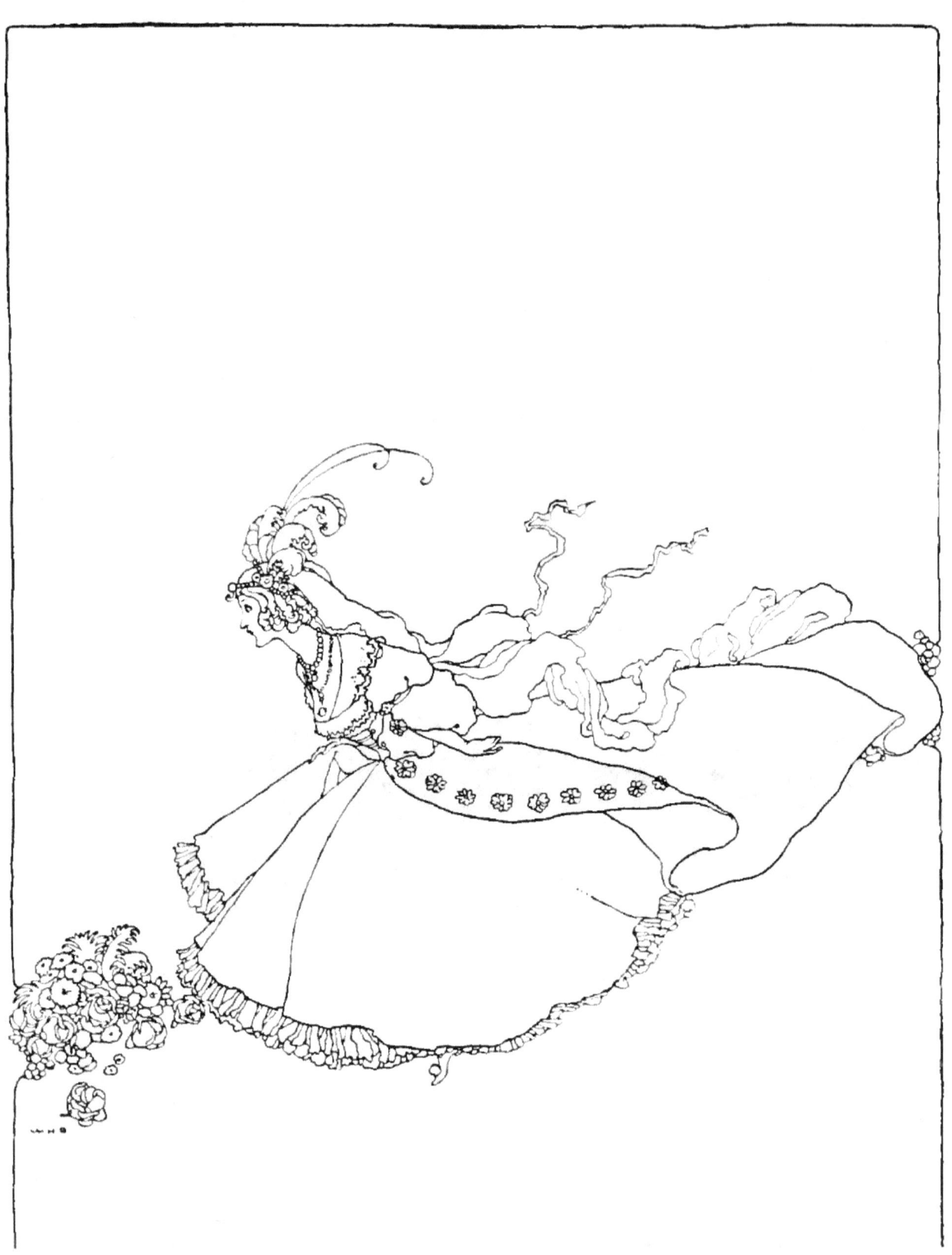

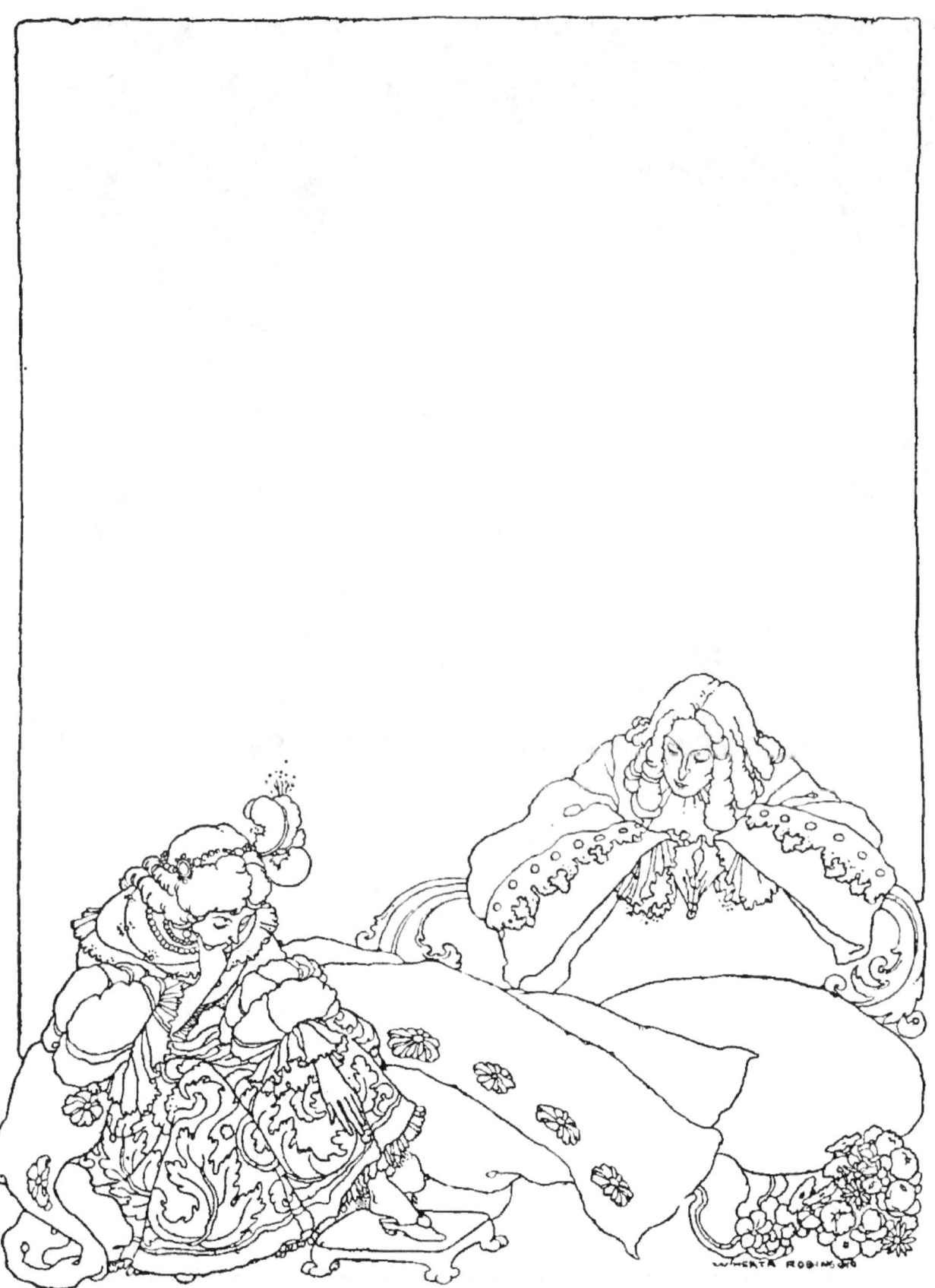

'*They tried it first on the princesses*'

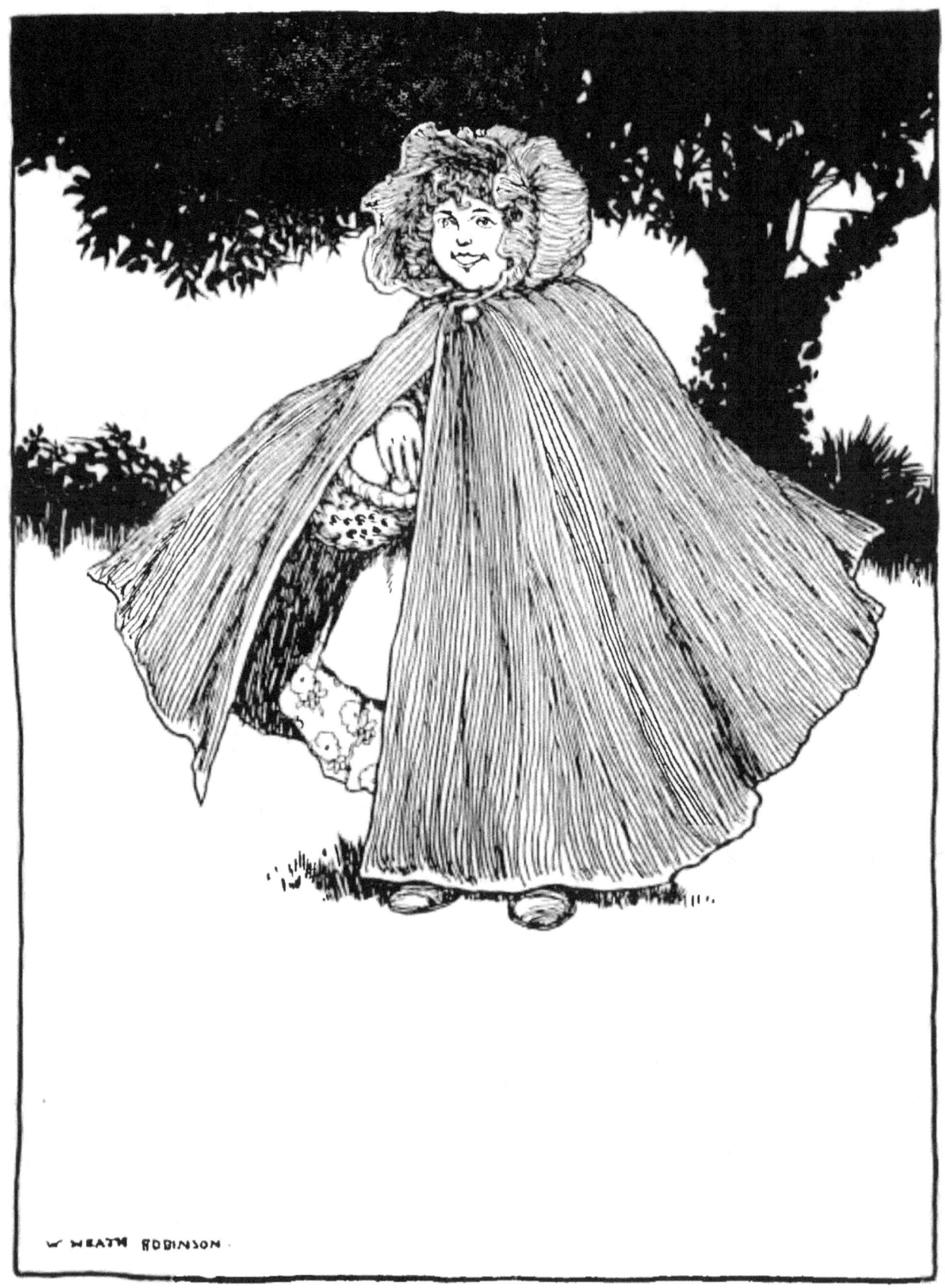

Little Red Riding Hood

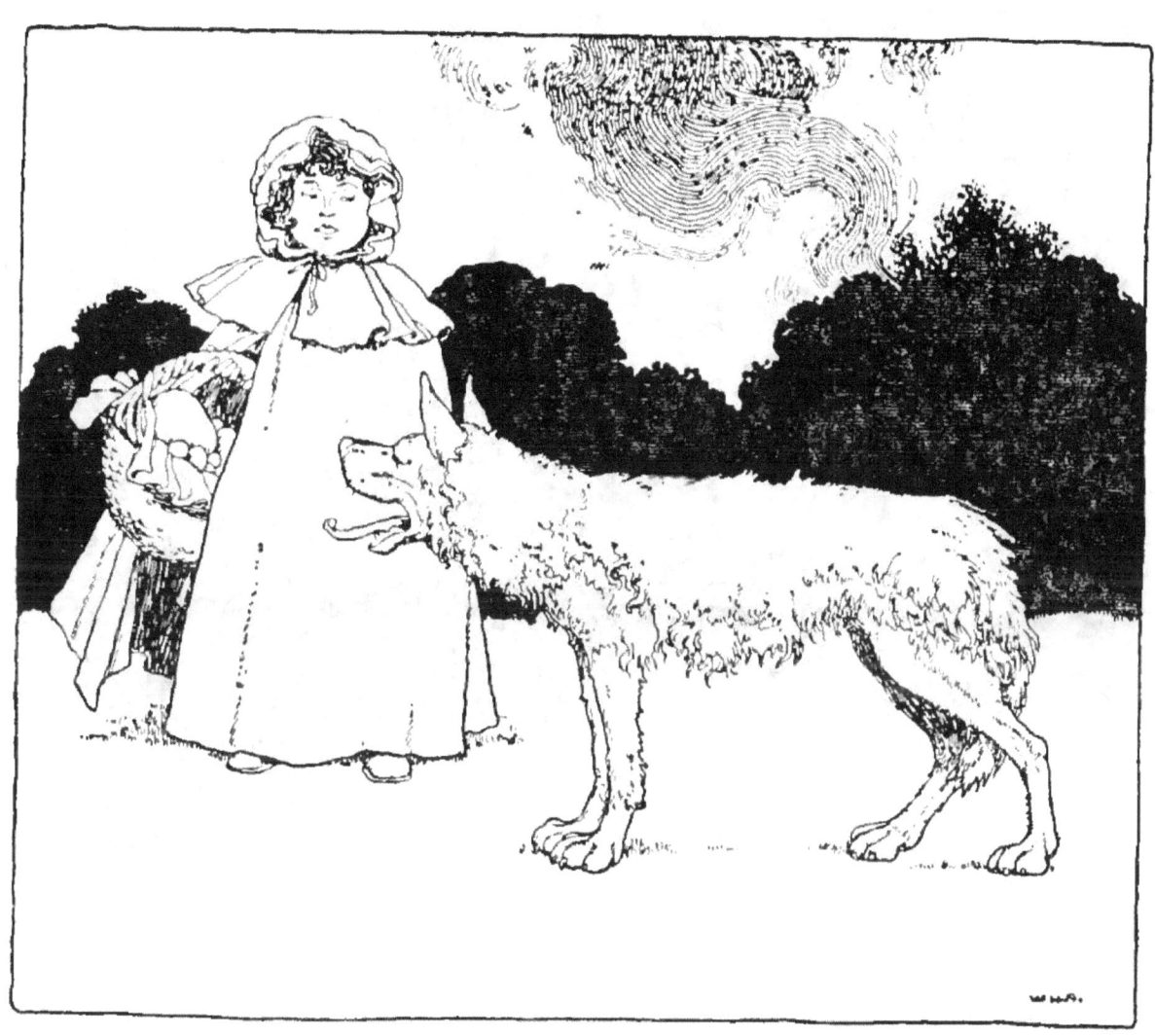

'She met old Father Wolf'

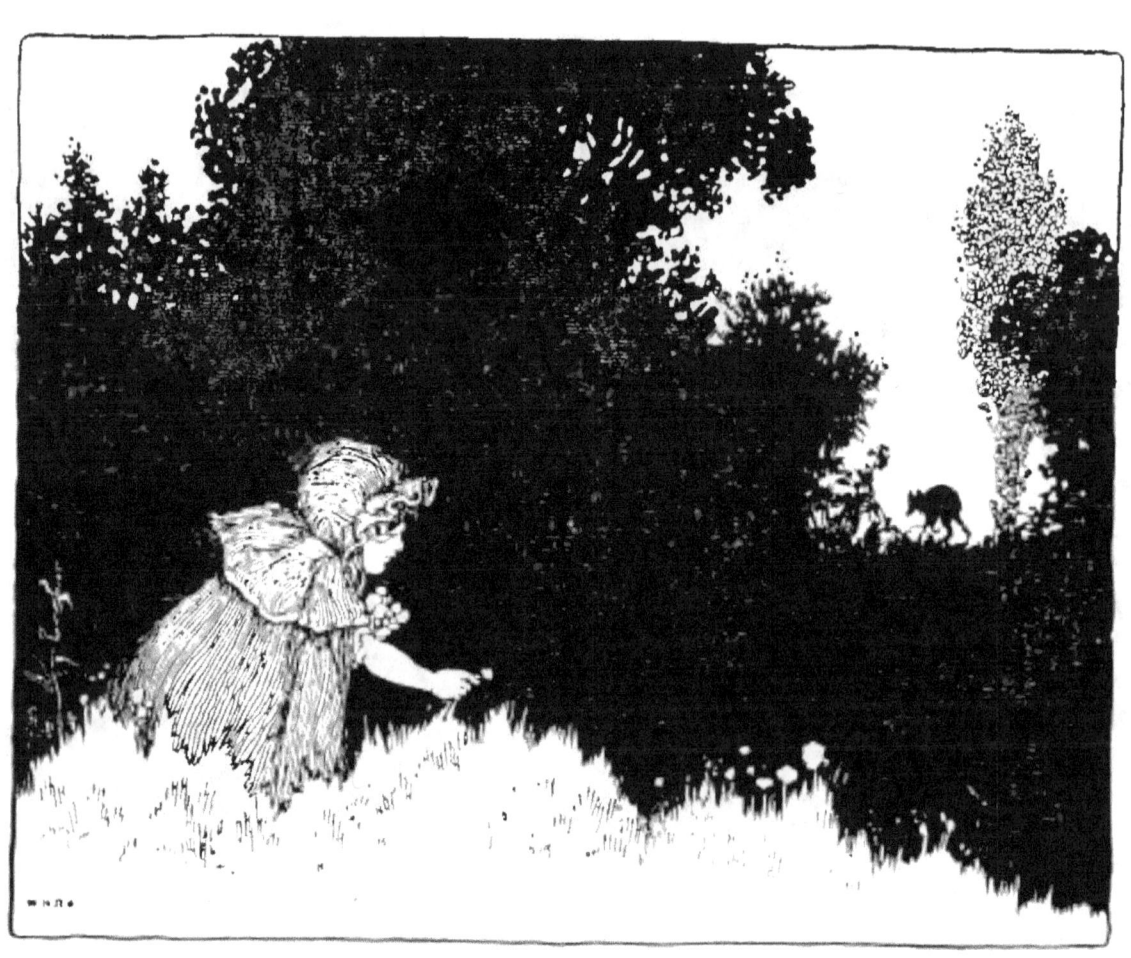

'*Making nosegays of the wild flowers*'

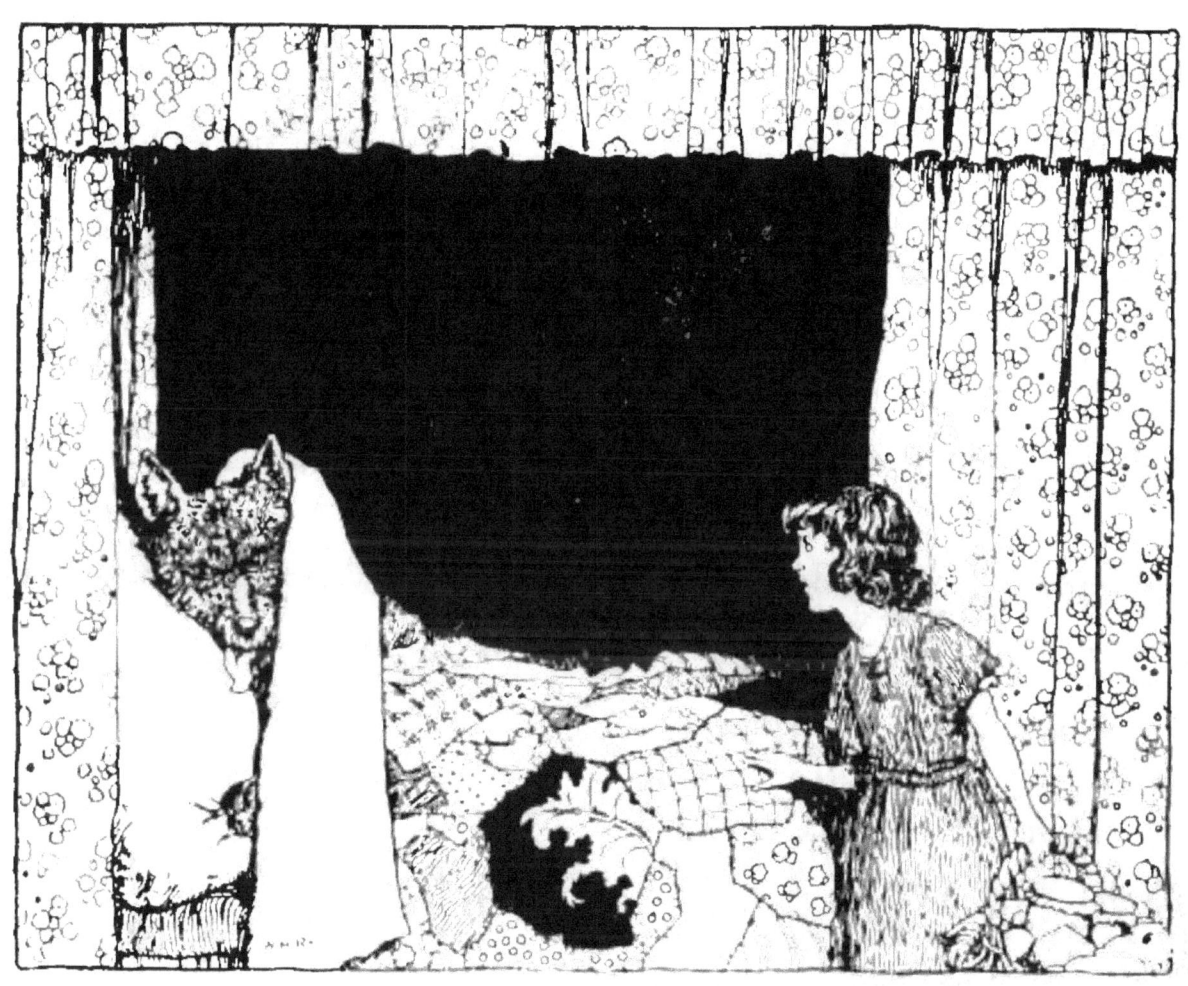

'Come up on the bed with me'

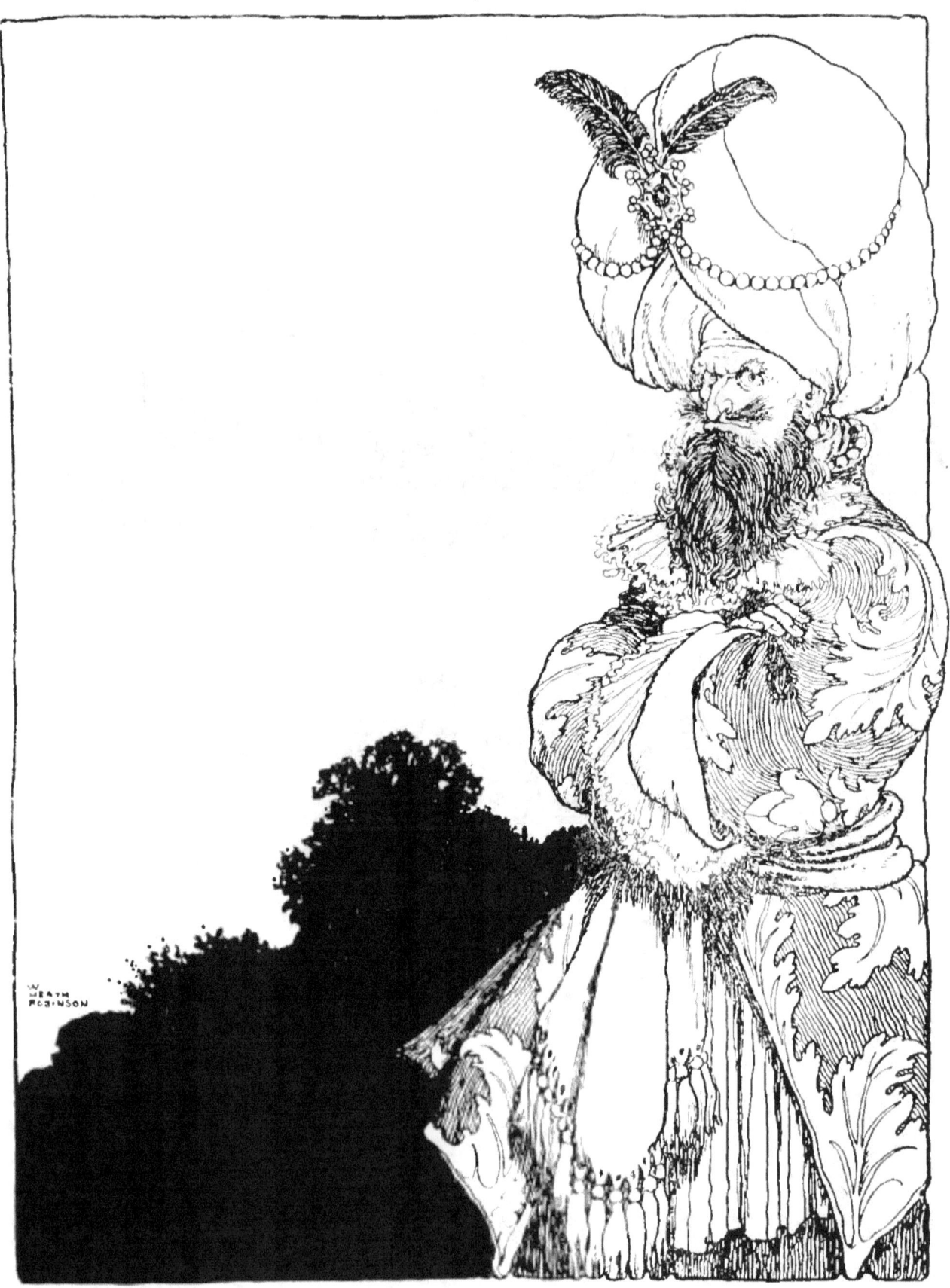

Blue Beard

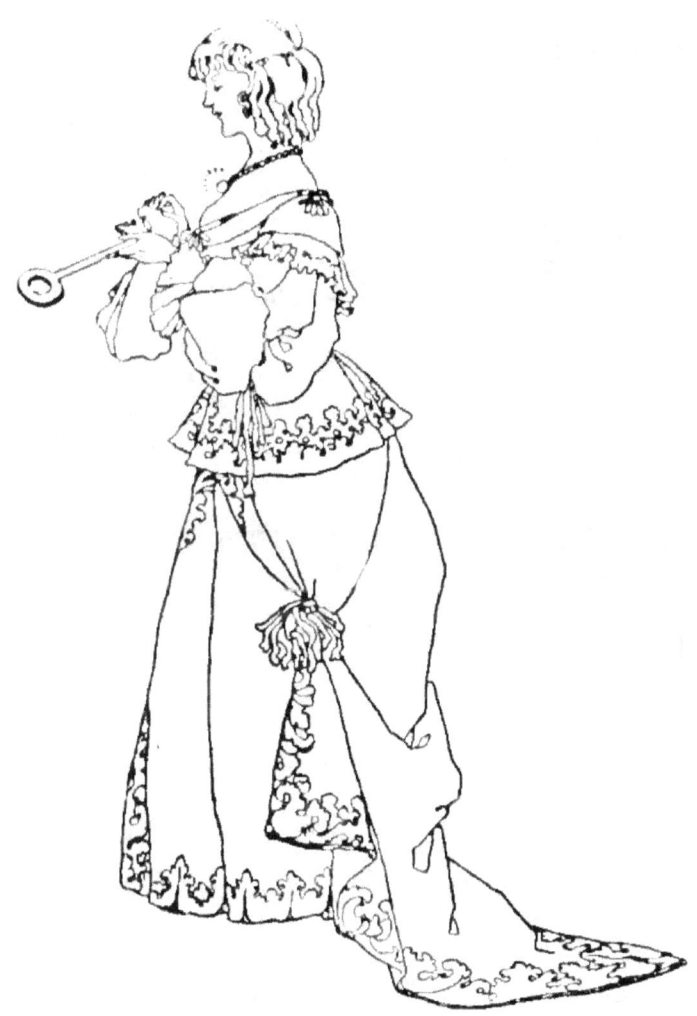

'*She washed it well*'

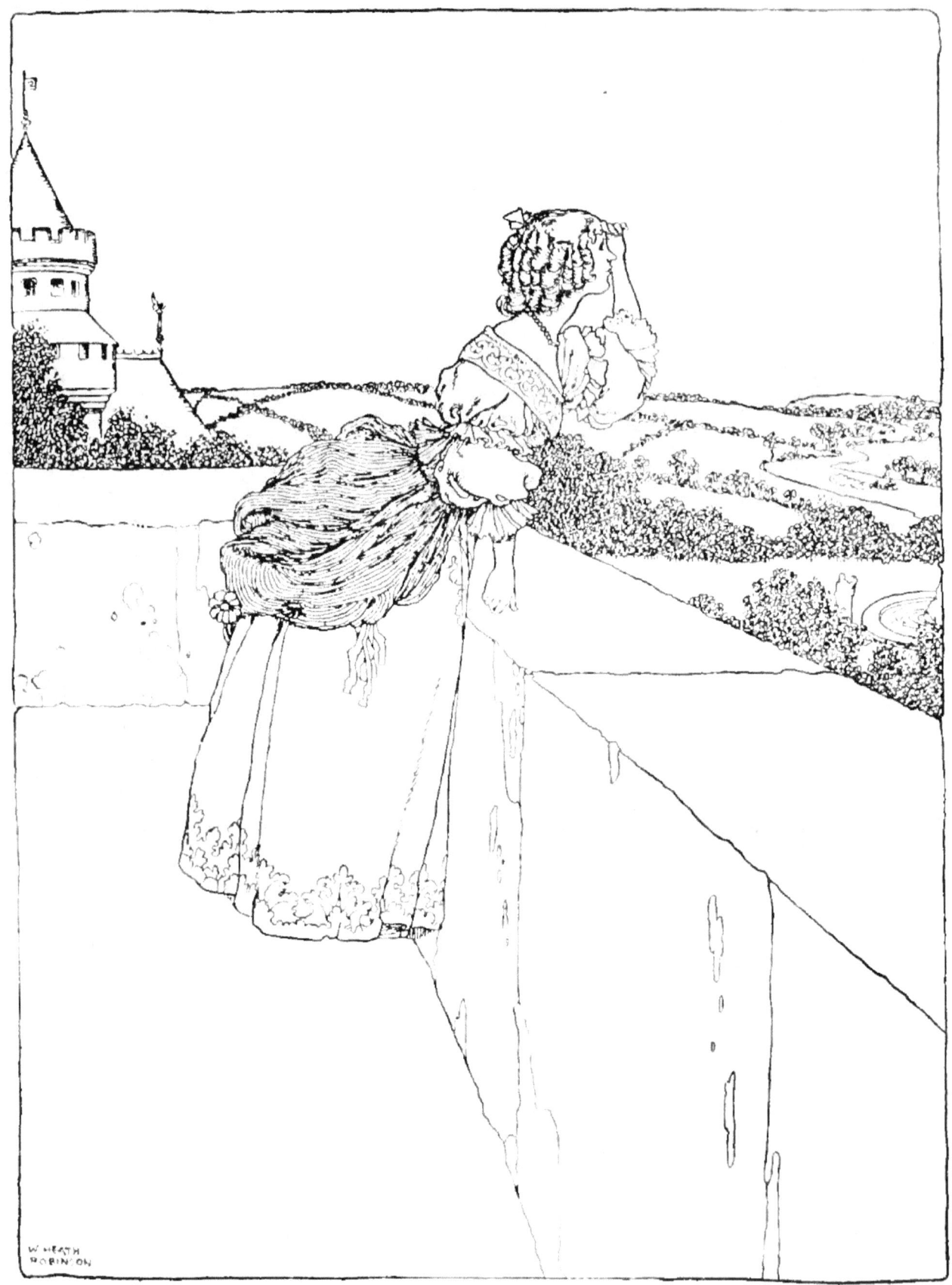

Sister Anne

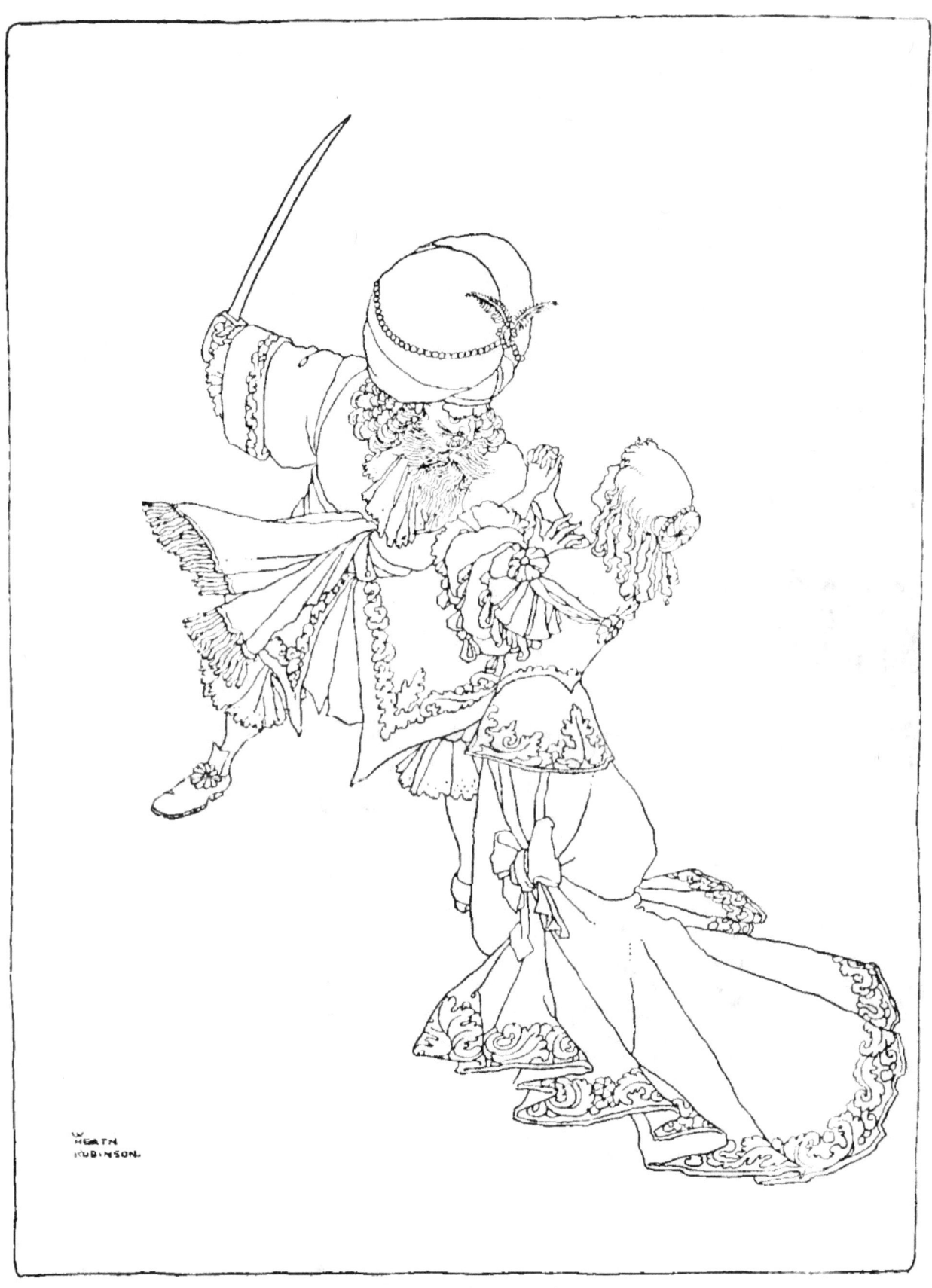

'Brandishing the cutlass aloft'

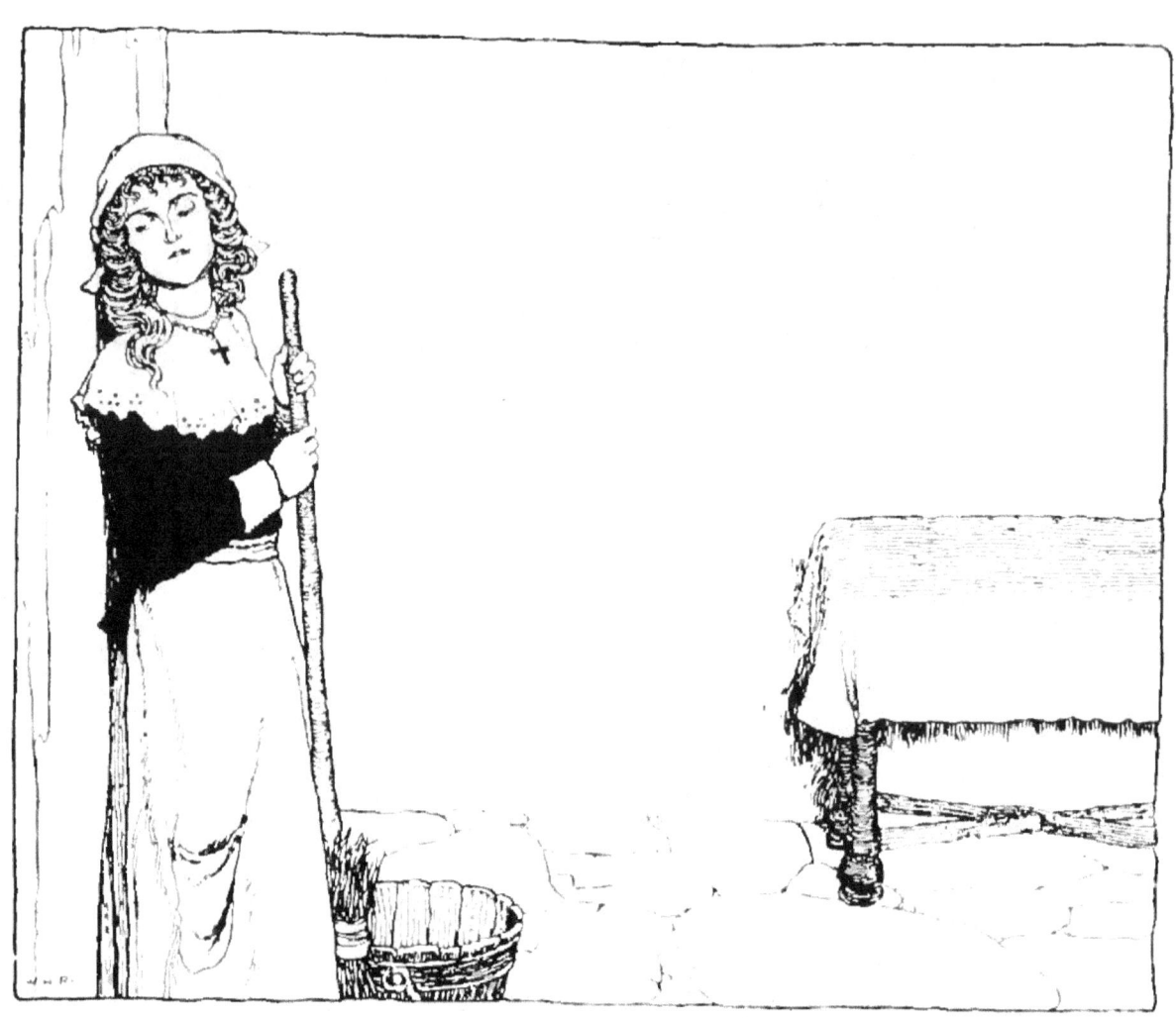

'At first she found it very hard'

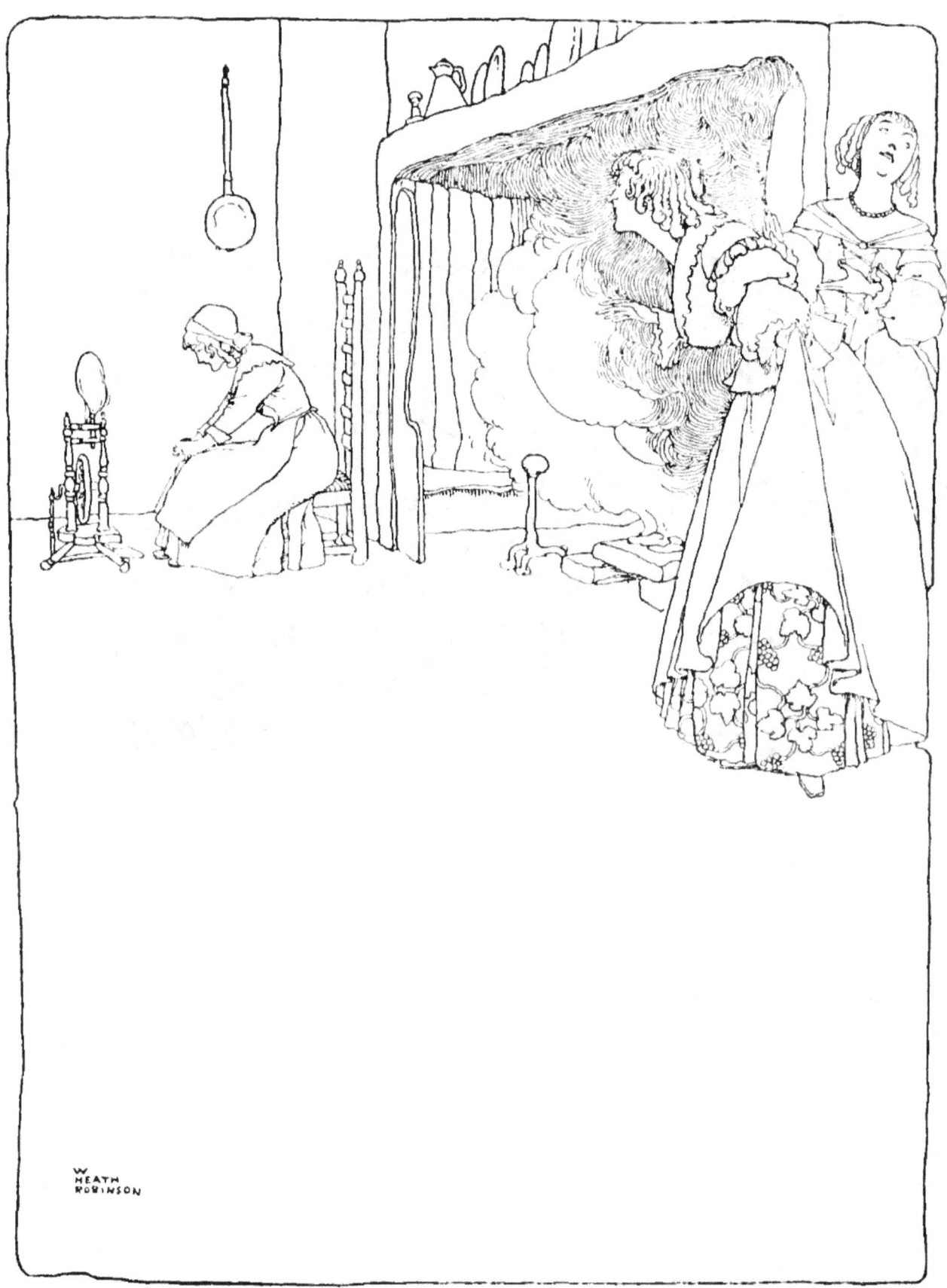

"Look at our little sister"

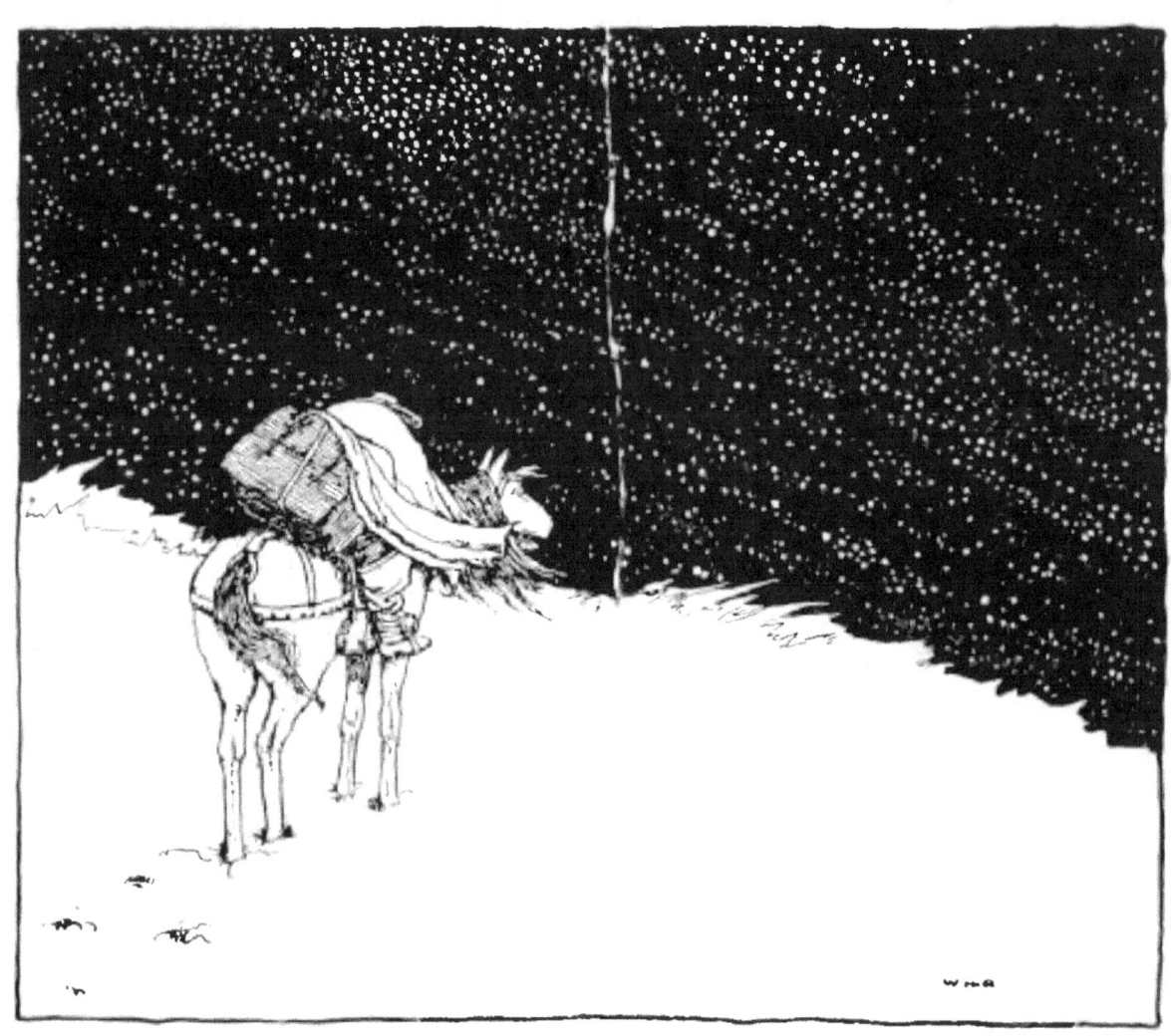

'It was snowing horribly'

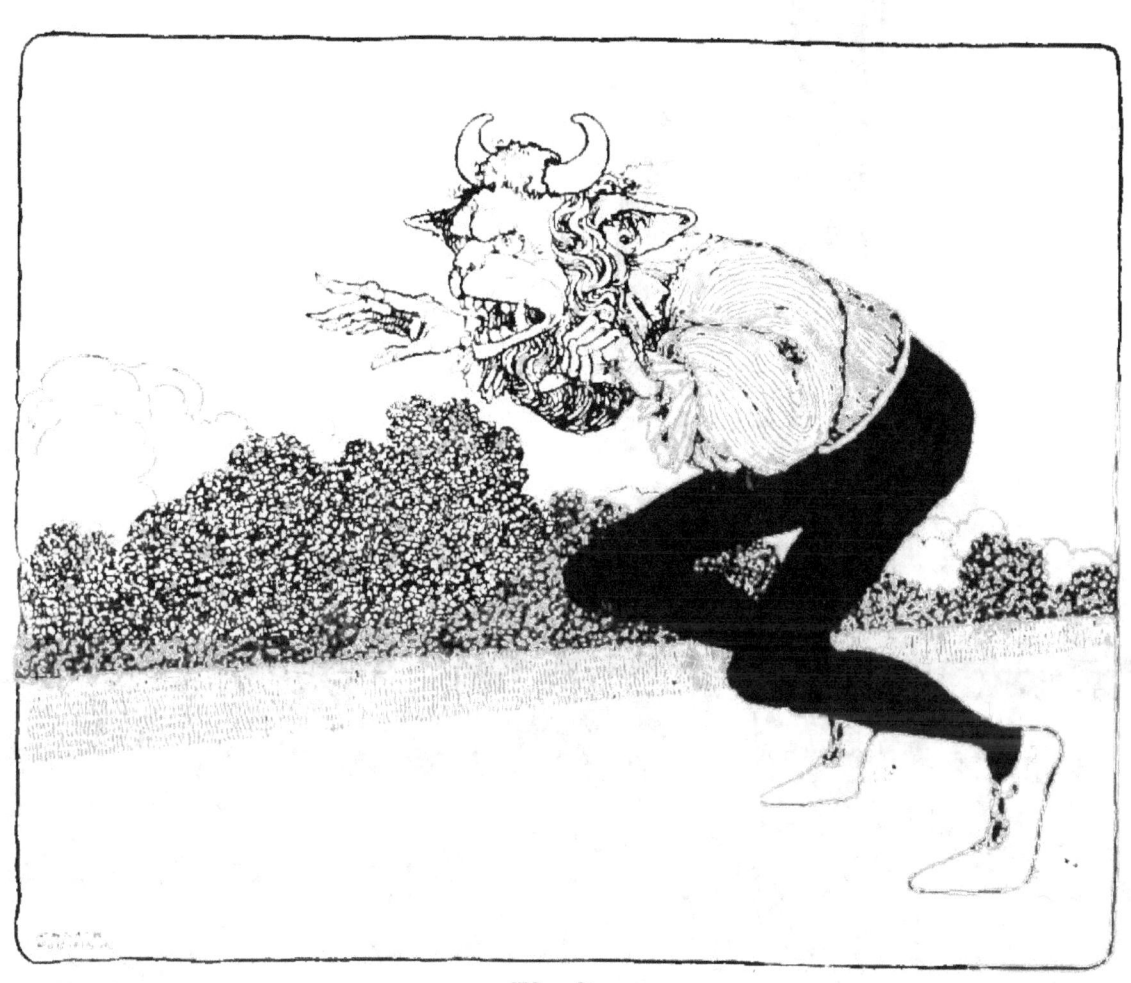
The Beast

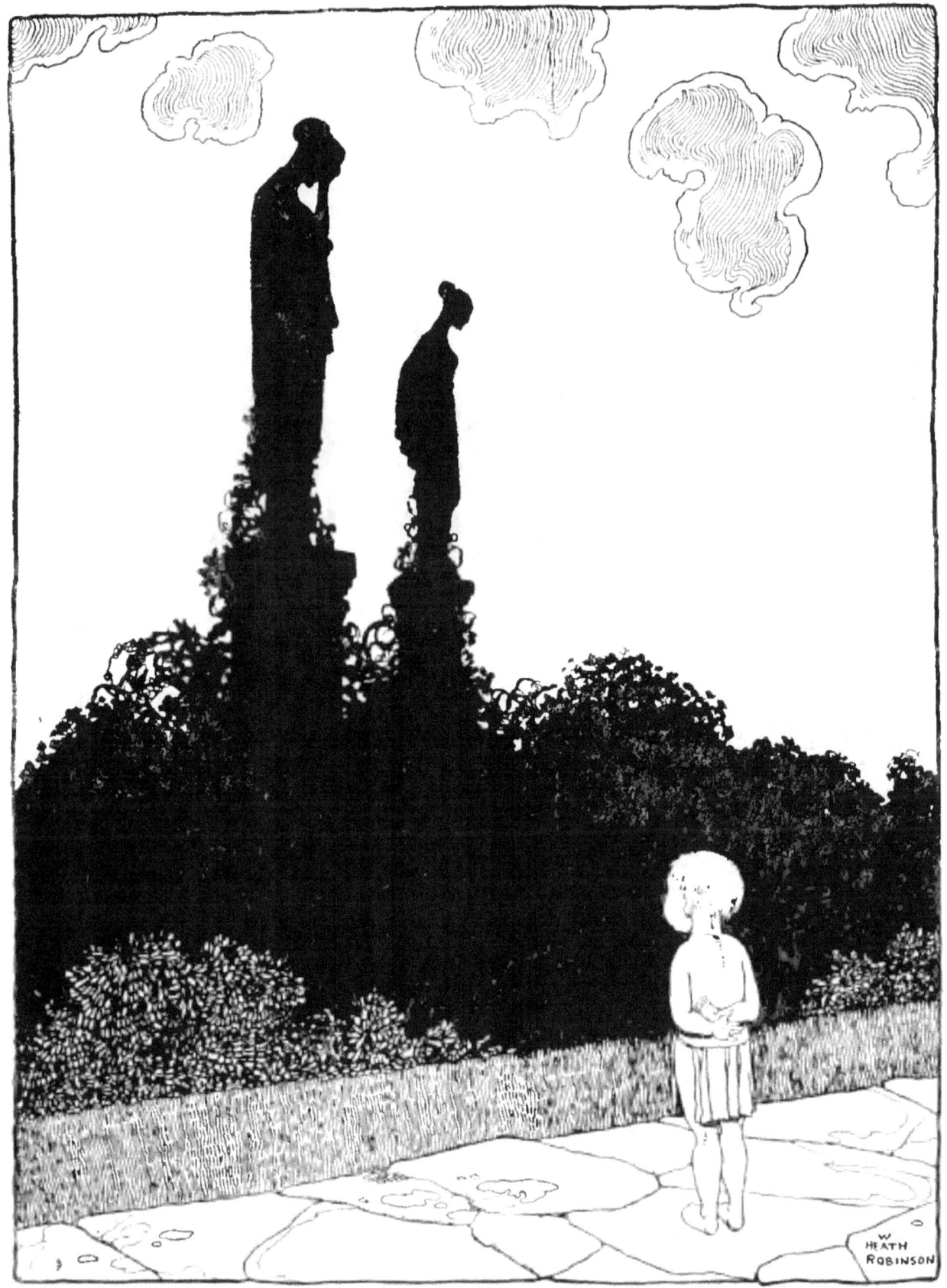

"Your doom is to become statues"

'The approach to it was by ten thousand steps'

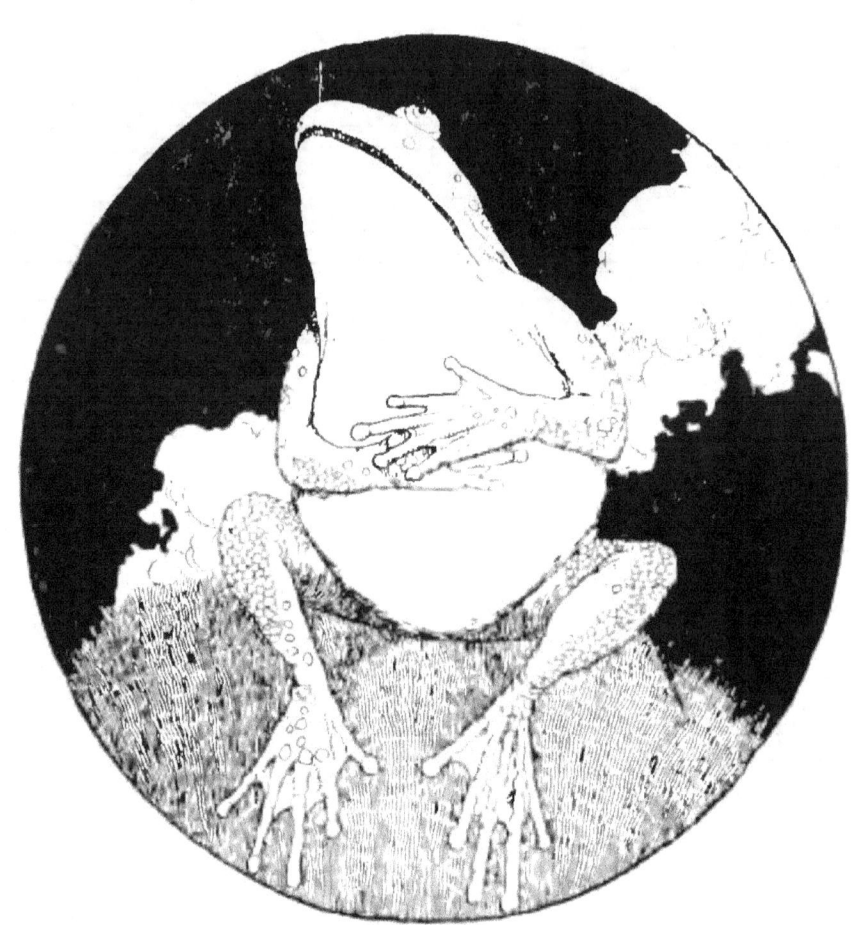

The Friendly Frog

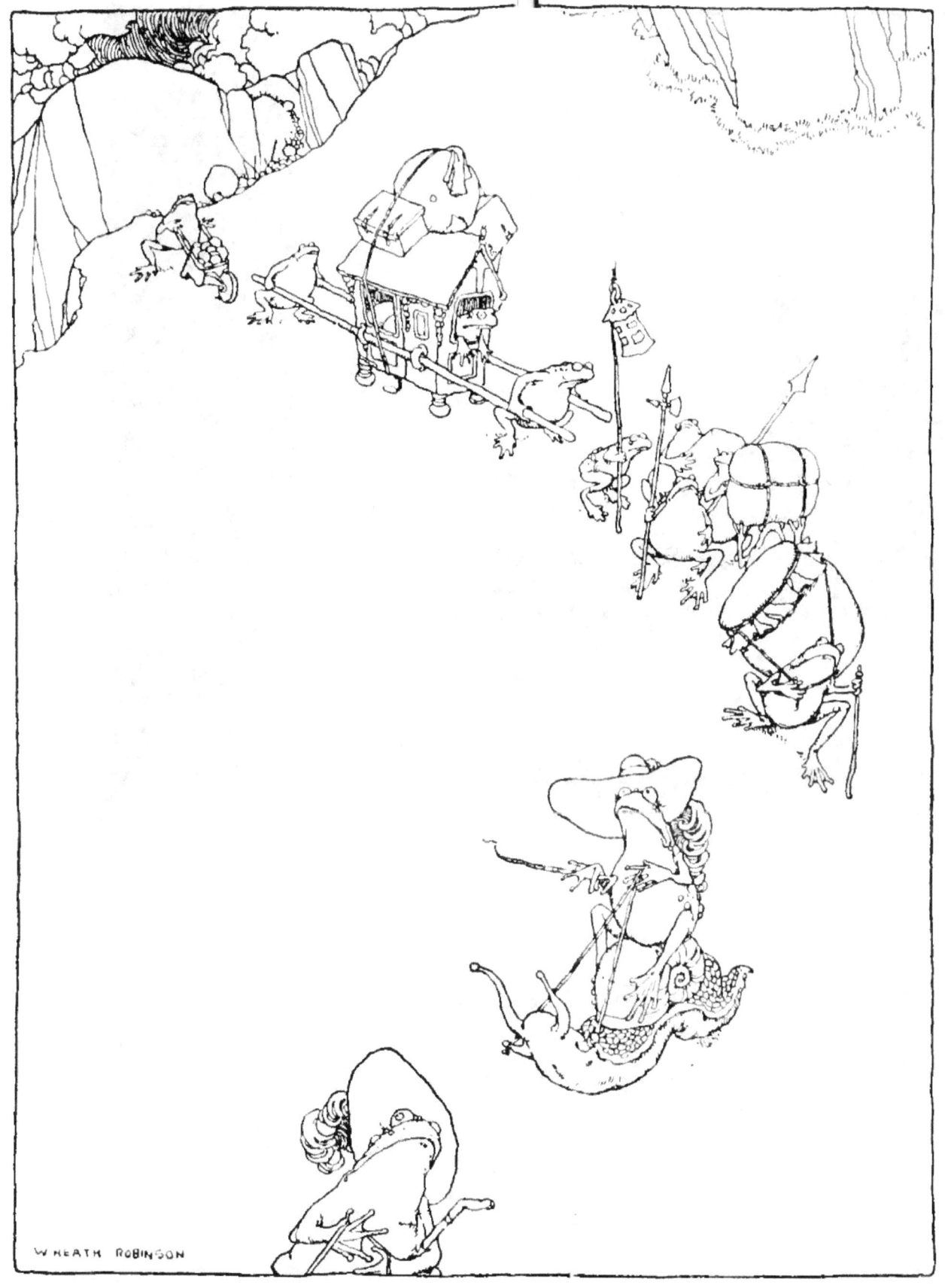

'The journey lasted seven years'

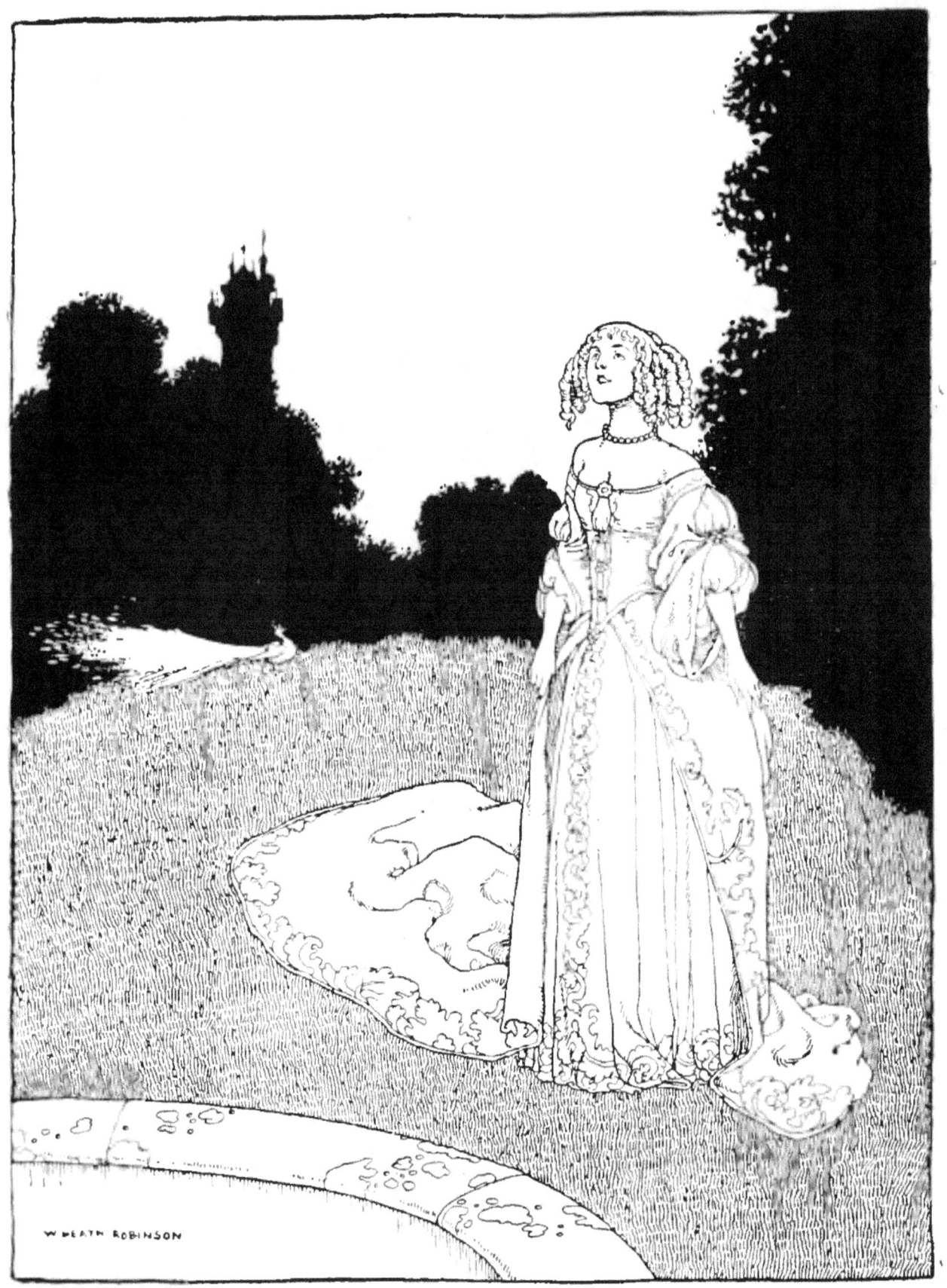

Princess Rosette

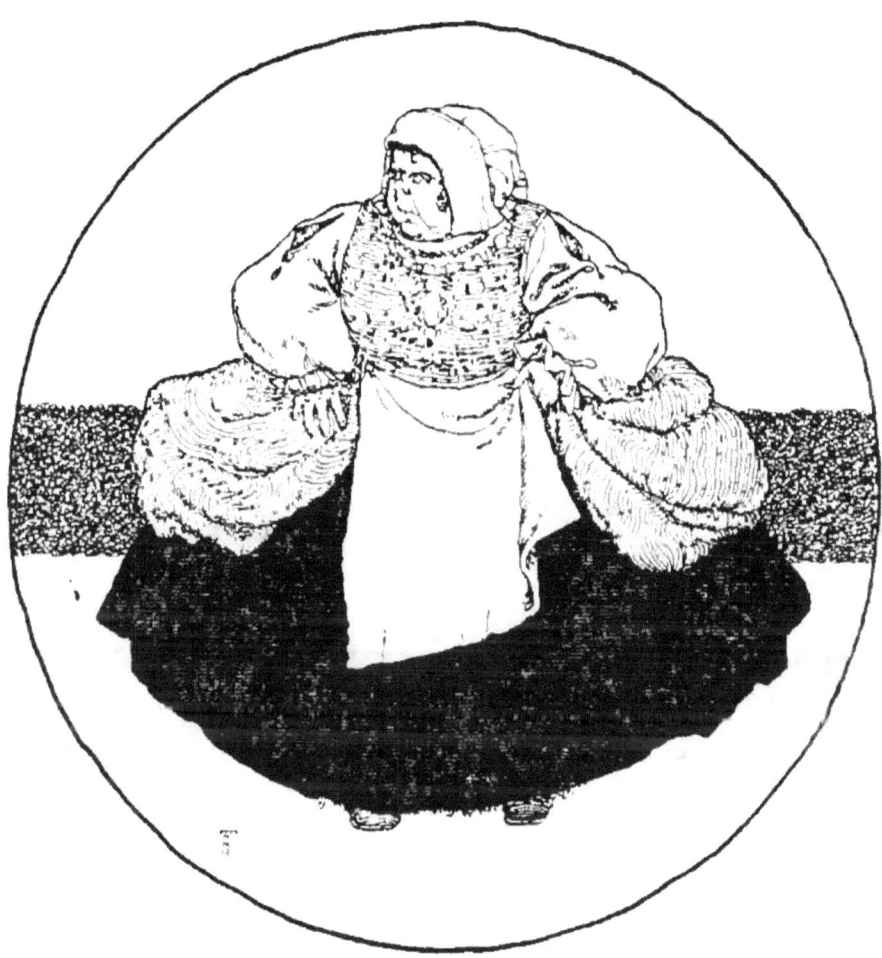

The wicked nurse

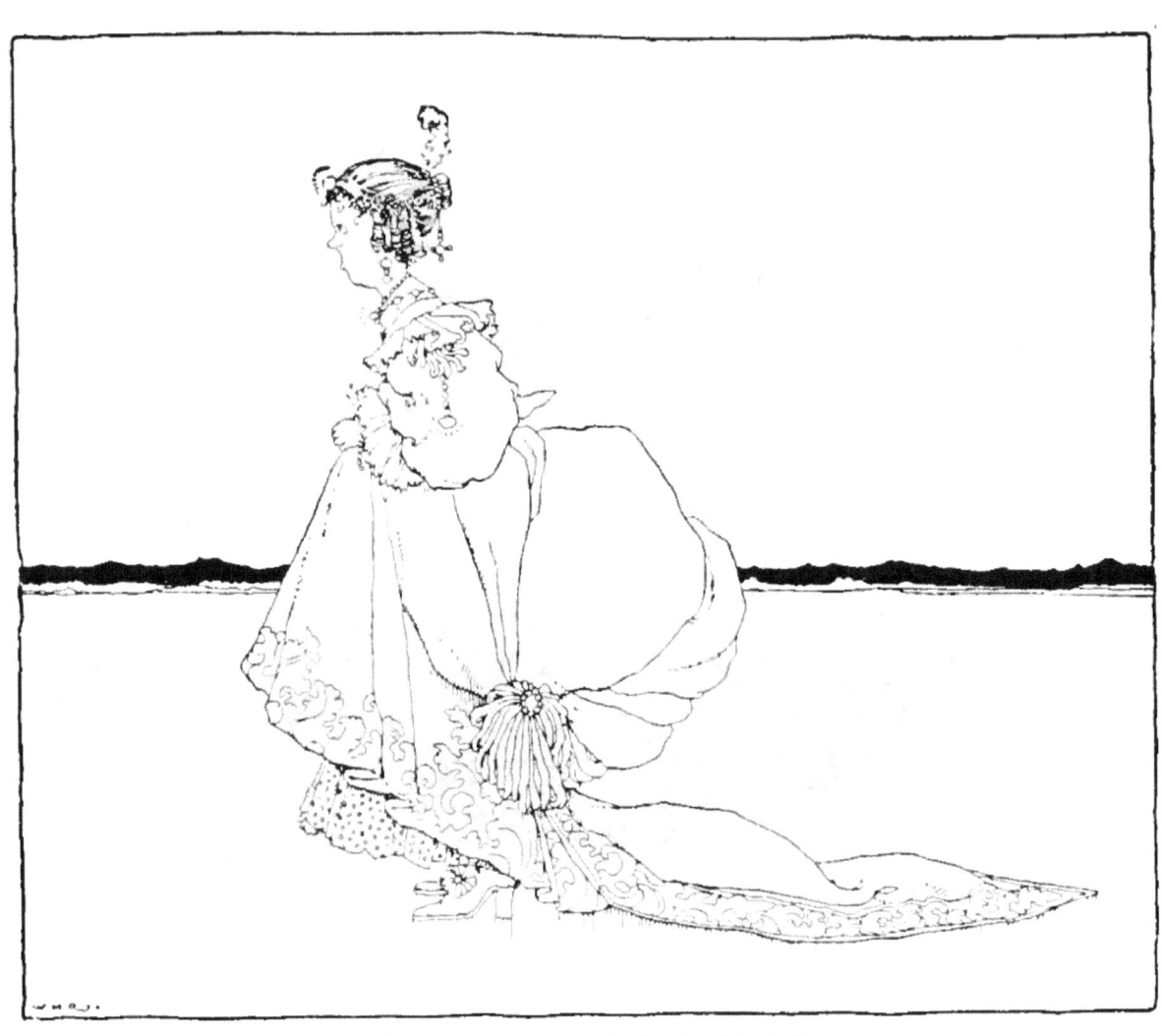

'*She was an ugly little fright*'

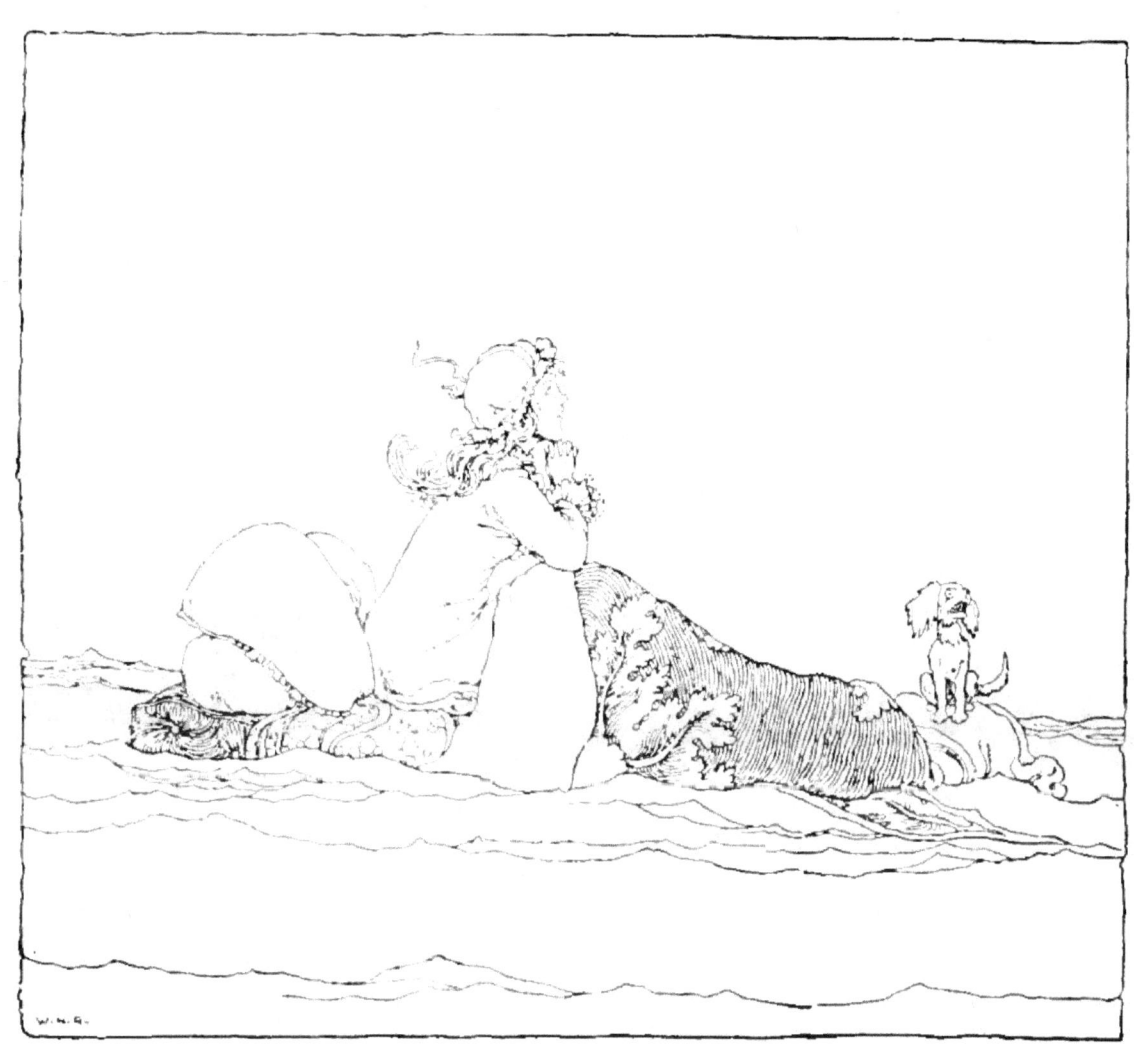

'*She floated hither and thither*'

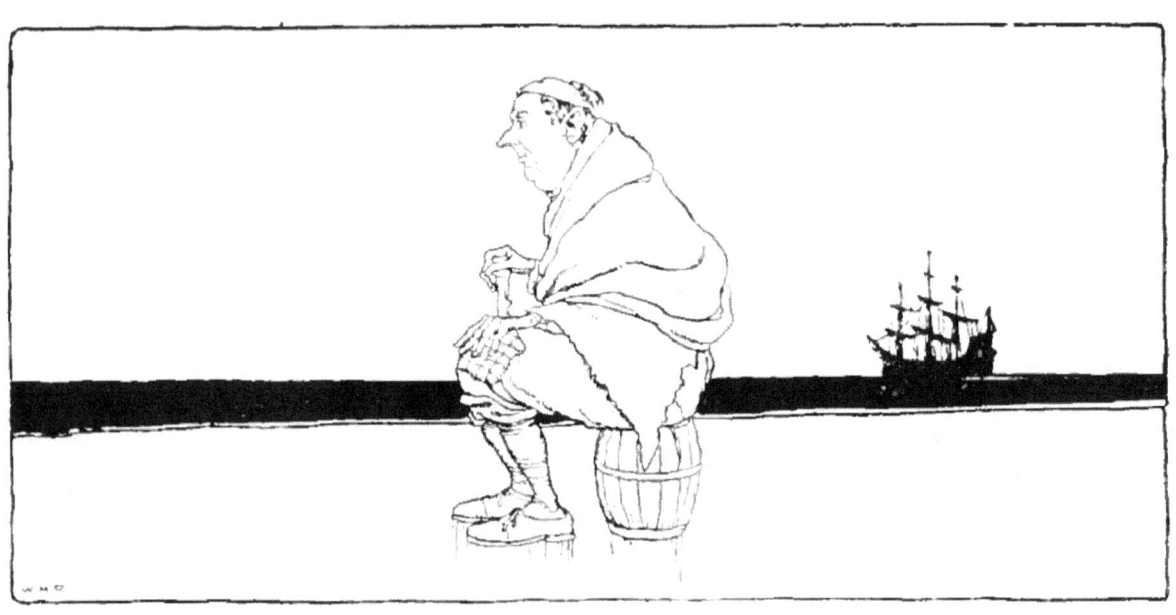

'*A kindly old man*'

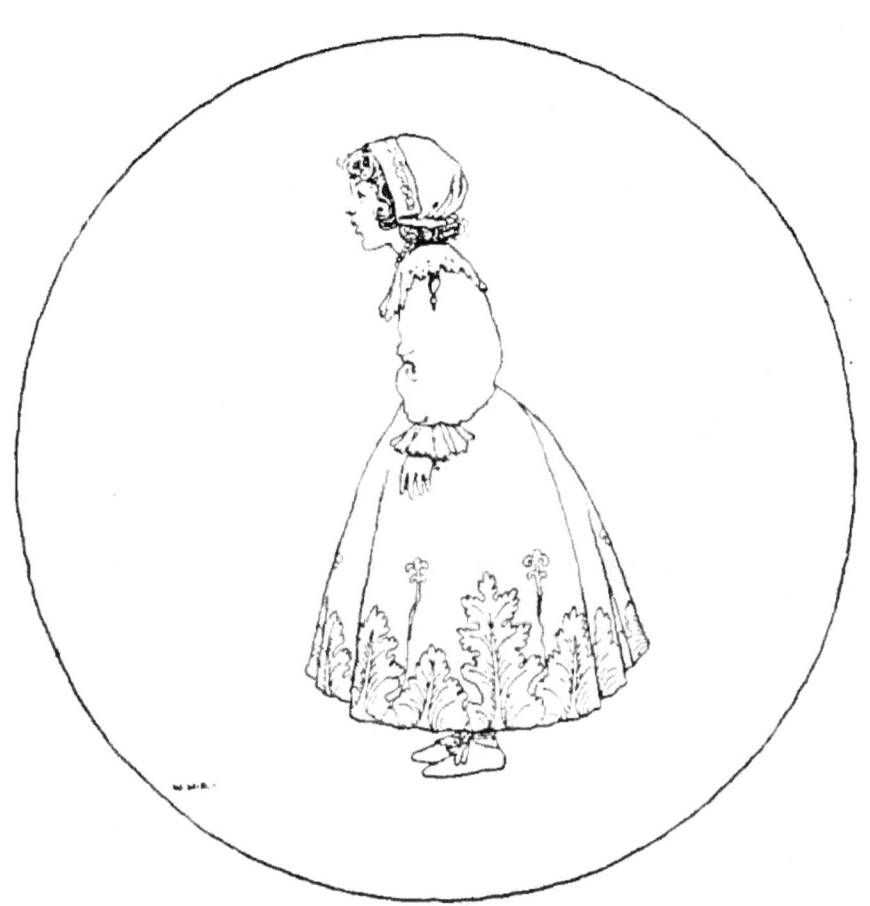

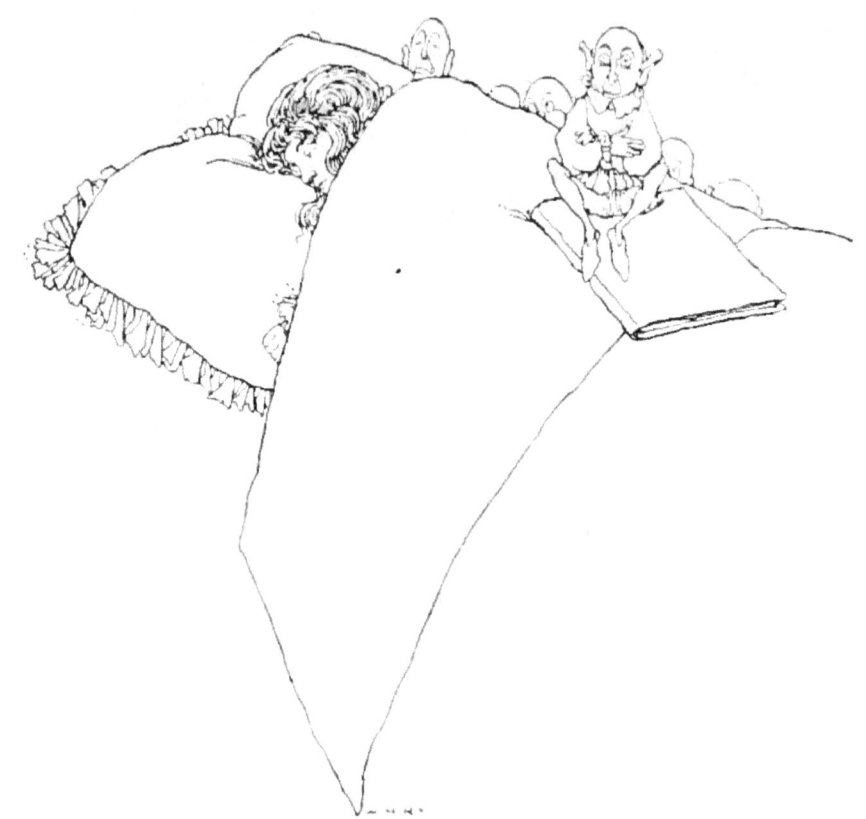

THE END